Index on Censorship

Free Word Centre, 60 Farringdon Road, London, ECIR 3GA

Chief Executive Kirsty Hughes **Deputy Chief Executive** Rohan Jayasekera **Editor** Jo Glanville **Finance Manager** David Sewell **Head of Events** Sara Rhodes **Online Editor** Emily Butselaar **News Editor** Padraig Reidy **Assistant Editor** Natasha Schmidt **Head of Advocacy** Michael Harris **Editorial Researcher** Marta Cooper **Head of Communications** Pam Cowburn **Programme Manager, Arts** Julia Farrington **Events Manager** Eve Jackson **Editorial Assistants** Alice Purkiss, Sara Yasin
Graphic designer Sam Hails
Cover design Brett Biedscheid
Printed by Page Bros., Norwich, UK

Volume 41 No 3 2012

If you are interested in republishing any article featured in this issue, please contact us at permissions@indexoncensorship.org

Supported using public funding by
ARTS COUNCIL ENGLAND
LOTTERY FUNDED

OPEN UNIVERSITIES

Jo Glanville

When the space for academic freedom shrinks, wider society suffers. As Thomas Docherty points out in a damning piece on the impact of the cuts in the UK, it is a freedom that is essential for exploring ideas that may challenge the status quo. Once academics become subservient to the state, whether through direct intimidation or the more subtle demands of funding, democracy itself is threatened: 'the university ... is an institution that will give an emergent democratic society its various identities, arguments and openness to future possibilities'.

In the UK, as Docherty demonstrates, academia has been progressively fenced in over the past 30 years: from the first demands for 'value for money', to the decision to make the higher education funding body accountable to government and the devastating withdrawal of funding from the arts, humanities and social sciences two years ago [pp46-54].

Elsewhere in the world, from Iraq to Belarus, there are other tactics to control academia. In Turkey, any scholar who goes near taboo topics (which include the Armenian genocide and the Kurds) risks their career and even their liberty. Maureen Freely examines the roots of academic censorship, which go back to the coup in 1980 and the founding of the Higher Education Council, whose members are appointed by the president. Academics are required to instil the 'national, moral, humanitarian, spiritual and cultural values of the Turkish nation'. Students and lecturers are fighting back against the current climate of intimidation in the face of prosecution and arrests [pp56-65].

In Thailand, academics are at the forefront of a recent challenge to a notorious chill on free speech: *lèse majesté*, which criminalises any insult to the king. A brave group of scholars led by Worachet Pakeerut – who has faced assault for daring to address the issue – has presented a draft amendment to the law in parliament. Since it is a law that goes to the heart of political struggle in Thailand, reform would mark a major sea change.

Turkish university students demonstrate against Turkey's Higher Education
Council on the anniversary of its formation, Istanbul University, 6 November 2007
Credit: Fatih Saribas/Reuters

THE ARAB REVOLUTIONS

WHAT YOU NEED TO KNOW

SATURDAY 15 SEPTEMBER

Did you follow Tahrir's 18 days? Do you care about Syria? What's really happening in the Arab world? Whether you think this is the spearhead of a global revolution, or you haven't thought much about it at all – this event is for you. Spend the day with activists and thinkers from the cutting edge of events, get up to the minute news and analysis and enjoy a great night out with the music of Eskenderella.

Hosted by Ahdaf Soueif and featuring Raja Shehadeh, Jamal Mahjoub, Omar Robert Hamilton, Maryam Al Khawaja, Salma Said, Sara Ishaq and many more.

Queen Elizabeth Hall and Foyer, 10am to 7pm
Day ticket: £12

Programme includes:

THE YEAR THAT CHANGED EVERYTHING
NEWS BRIEFINGS FROM
THE REVOLUTIONS
Tunisia, Egypt, Libya, Syria, Yemen,
Bahrain and Sudan
Hosted and moderated by Ahdaf Soueif

ANOTHER BRICK IN THE WALL
TRANSNATIONAL TACTICS
OF REPRESSION
Talk and Screening

FALLEGA 2011
(UK PREMIERE)
Talk and screening with Q and A with director Rafik Omrani. Shortly after President Ben Ali fled Tunisia, the first revolutionary sit-in began. This is its story.

ORDERING PIZZA FOR WISCONSIN FROM TAHRIR

FRONTLINE AVANT-GARDE
THE ARTIST IN THE REVOLUTION

NEXT YEAR IN JERUSALEM?
PALESTINE AND THE ARAB REVOLUTIONS

TAHRIR CINEMA
Ongoing screenings of short videos and films made by resident journalists and filmmakers.

LIVE GIG: ESKENDERELLA
Hear the music of the revolution. Eskenderella travelled all over Egypt performing in public gatherings, protests, sit-ins, factories and universities, and became the biggest and the most popular Egyptian band of the revolution.

Queen Elizabeth Hall, 8.30pm
£15 (separate ticket to day event)

Due to the continuously changing nature of the region, the curator reserves the right to make changes and alterations to the programme.

TICKETS 0844 847 9910
SOUTHBANKCENTRE.CO.UK

SOUTHBANK CENTRE

Index also explores the changing face of academic publishing in this issue, as two researchers from different fields of scholarship put the case for open access: the availability of research can save lives as well as advance knowledge [pp115-126].

This autumn will be an important moment for press freedom in the UK, as the Leveson Inquiry into the culture, practices and ethics of the media prepares to publish its report and the defamation bill goes through its final stages – marking the end of a three-year campaign in which Index has played a leading role with its partners English PEN and Sense about Science. Five leading players outline their hopes and expectations of Leveson in this issue and Mark Henderson revisits the pivotal role played by the science geeks in the libel reform campaign. We're also delighted to publish former *Index* editor Andrew Graham-Yooll's report on recent revelations about Argentina's dirty war and Malu Halasa on her remarkable exhibition on Syrian artists' response to the uprising. In our continuing celebration of *Index*'s 40th, we're republishing an interview with Harold Pinter about his controversial poem on the Gulf War, and an essay by Arthur Miller first published in 1978.

This is my last issue as editor. It's been a privilege to edit a magazine with such a remarkable literary and political heritage, and to work with so many talented and courageous writers over the last five years. May it flourish for at least another 40. ❏

©Jo Glanville
41(3): 1/4
DOI: 10.1177/0306422012457135
www.indexoncensorship.org

CONTENTS

LAST WORD

Rallying against budget cuts in education, Ann Arbor, Michigan, USA, 30 April 2011
Credit: Jim West/Alamy

DISPATCHES

What we want from Leveson:
Guido Fawkes, Trevor Kavanagh
and more on the future of press freedom

From the archive: Pinter on censorship

What the geeks did for libel reform

Protest during the Leveson Inquiry at the Royal Courts of Justice, 24 April 2012
Credit: Maciek Musialek/Demotix

JOURNALISM IN THE DOCK

Marta Cooper looks back at Leveson. **Trevor Kavanagh**, **Guido Fawkes**, **Mark Lewis**, **Martin Moore** and **Alan Rusbridger** reflect on the future

It began with the hacking of an abducted schoolgirl's phone. In July 2011, the *Guardian* revealed that Milly Dowler's mobile phone had been hacked by the *News of the World* around the time of her disappearance in March 2002, triggering a public outcry, the closure of the Sunday tabloid itself and the setting up of the Leveson Inquiry to examine press ethics, culture and practices. While the Metropolitan and Surrey police forces have since revealed that it is impossible to say with any certainty that the tabloid deleted the messages that caused the teenager's family to have false hope she was alive, it is uncontested that the paper accessed her voicemails. The police have not been able to pin down what caused the messages on Milly's phone to clear.

The first weeks of evidence confirmed what we knew: of course the tabloids use underhand methods to get stories. Paps camping outside the homes of celebrities and ordinary citizens? Unsurprising. An unfaithful celebrity cultivating the 'family man' image? Red-top fodder.

Yet despite the appetite for scandal in our culture – 'the last big throw-back to Victorian England', to quote former chief secretary to the Treasury and kiss-and-tell victim David Mellor – the British public was rarely present at the inquiry.

It often felt as if journalism was in the dock. In May, *Independent on Sunday* editor John Mullin was summoned to explain how he had sourced a story that, the inquiry claimed, contained elements from Andy Coulson's witness statement, which was not yet public. An unwavering Mullin explained that the story was down to 'good honest journalism' based on three independent sources, but that didn't stop some grandstanding from counsel David Barr, who continued to press Mullin. No further action was taken by Leveson on the matter, but at that moment the gulf between journalists and the inquiry's lawyers had never seemed quite so vast.

Moments of chill also spiralled into ridicule. Simon Walters of the *Mail on Sunday* was asked by a confident Carine Patry-Hoskins whether using the words 'at last' in a headline represented a degree of comment or opinion. Walters, unsure if he had any involvement with the online version of the article in question, said it was 'pretty mild' by way of comment.

Crime reporters also grew exasperated as they had to explain social engagements with police officers – lunch, coffee, dinner, whether or not alcohol was involved – with many lamenting that previously open channels of communication had been shut down in the wake of the inquiry.

But for all its sometimes excessive scrutiny and theatrics, this inquiry matters because the future of the British press is in its hands. It is a matter of weeks before LJL recommends a new regulatory system. Various suggestions have been put to him: a press-card model, a contractual system, a body able to fine errant newspapers up to £1 million and a system backed by legislation to resolve privacy cases.

Calls against statutory regulation have been boisterous, although several titles have said they see the possibility for statutory underpinning of a new system. With onlookers unable to predict his thinking, Leveson has said any fears of censorship or curbing our cherished press freedom are misplaced.

Misplaced or not, there is a strong personal and professional investment in the outcome. John Lloyd put it best in the *Financial Times* when he described how the press had developed in a way that was 'organically bohemian, anti-authoritarian, possibly over-emotional . . . but nevertheless free'.

There was, he said, an attachment to retaining 'the right to be irresponsible', which might explain aversions to the more stringent regulation that binds the legal and medical professions.

Exposed illegality is being dealt with, and rightly so. But it comes back to culture: unethical newsroom practices flourished because they could; only stronger editorial governance can deal with them. But this must be balanced by public interest defences across the array of criminal offences that apply to the media.

If the state regulates the press, then the press, to quote Ian Hislop, 'no longer regulates the state'. Perhaps there are nuances Leveson can find in his new system, but he, unlike the journalists his recommendations will affect, will not have to deal with the emotional fallout.

Marta Cooper is editorial researcher at Index on censorship and reported on the Leveson Inquiry

Squaring the circle by Guido Fawkes

So far Lord Justice Leveson has been angry with me, threatened me with jail, censored me, twice summoned me, argued with me at his inquiry and thrice ordered me to write for him – unpaid – 5,000 words so far.

To be fair, I did publish Alastair Campbell's evidence before he gave it to the inquiry and ignored Leveson's subsequent stern orders to keep evidence to the inquiry secret, publishing all the bits of the Operation Motorman files [information commissioner's investigation into data protection breaches] that I could get my hands on. I also told him to his face that his inquiry will be judged a failure if no journalists named in the Operation Motorman investigation files are prosecuted – something Leveson disputes in a hand-wringing legal decision not to advise in favour of the prosecution of hundreds of illegal information blagging journalists.

Leveson has been given a tough job – squaring the press freedom circle with a public sense that the tabloids went too far with phone hacking and info blagging. Not forgetting that the broadsheets still want to be able to do a little bit of hacking and info blagging when it is in the public interest as determined by themselves. Nobody wants judicial or political control of the newspapers, and nobody is really convinced that the ferociously competitive tabloids will restrain themselves in the long run.

My initial opinion of Leveson was that the prime minister appointed him to make sure that all the media groups got it in the neck, not just News International – that is still my view of the politics of it all. Leveson and Jay have in my view figured out what has been going on and are far from naive. Self-important hacks like to jump on any evidence of lack of knowledge of their ink-stained ways to prove how they are misunderstood. When it came out that the inquiry lawyers had not realised that sub-editors wrote headlines, hacks were quickly tweeting self-satisfied harrumphs to the effect that no meaningful informed reform was possible because the lawyers didn't even know journalists were not responsible for the headlines above their

The Dowler family's solicitor Mark Lewis gives a press statement following Rupert Murdoch's apology, London, 15 July 2011
Credit: Prixnews/Alamy

by-lines. Hacks resent the whole process and the chilling effect it is having on press freedom. For example, my own sideline in broking political scandal stories to the Sunday tabloids is experiencing a bit of recession as editors fear to rock the boat at this sensitive period for the press.

Where will this all end? Leveson will recommend some sort of beefed up successor to the Press Complaints Commission. It may or may not have a statutory underpinning, something that I think should be avoided because legislation will inevitably lead to judges becoming censors. My admittedly minority view is that we don't need more regulations or regulators; the hacking of Milly Dowler was illegal, information blagging was illegal, we just need to enforce the laws we have.

None of the forthcoming regulations will make a blind bit of difference to me. I realised early on that the British libel laws were too oppressive and based the Guido Fawkes Blog site offshore from the outset. Lord Black's draft proposal on behalf of media proprietors for a contractually based regulator is not even designed to govern offshore sites like mine. In truth it would be in my commercial interest and distinct competitive advantage to see the British media heavily regulated, draconian privacy laws enacted and politically correct 'media standards' enforced. All of which I would cheerfully ignore. It would, however, be a sad day for press freedom.

The Guido Fawkes Blog is edited by its founder, **Paul Staines**

With power comes responsibility by Martin Moore

There is no shortage of quotes or aphorisms about the corrupting nature of too much power. From Thomas Bailey's warning that 'The possession of unlimited power will make a despot of almost any man' to Lord Acton's 'absolute power corrupts absolutely'. Why does this happen? Empathy, as readers of Machiavelli's *The Prince* will know, can be detrimental to the pursuit of power. 'It is much safer,' Machiavelli wrote, 'to be feared than to be loved.' Powerful people, in other words, can cease to see other people as human.

This appears to be what happened at parts of News International, where the subjects of stories – whether they were politicians, celebrities, public fig-ures or the victims of a tragedy – were harassed, hounded, intimidated and discarded. It reached such a scale – the victims of phone hacking number in the thousands – because News International accumulated enormous power, and this power went almost entirely unchecked.

The Leveson Inquiry has laid out the consequences of such unchecked power. Individuals' lives turned over, scarred, and – in the case of some victims – irreparably damaged. Swathes of public life corrupted. The political process distorted and prostituted. The most important result of the inquiry therefore has to be checks on this power. Sensible and pro-portionate ways of making these big media corporations responsible for their actions.

The media corporations will argue – indeed already have – that any checks on their power equate to constraints on their freedom of expression. This is disingenuous and misleadingly blurs the line between a corpora-tion's power to say and do what it likes, and an individual's right to free speech.

Individual speech and corporate speech are not the same thing. As Professor Onora O'Neill said in her 2011 Reuters Institute lecture at Oxford:

(continues on p.22)
Credit: Andrew Thomson/Sector 4 Illustration

The Leveson Effect

What should the inquiry do? As little as possible, suggests **Trevor Kavanagh.** The press does not need licences like dogs and gun owners

Lord Justice Leveson is said by those who know him to regret taking on David Cameron's ill-conceived inquiry into press ethics. But not as much as the newspaper industry into whose inner workings he is delving with such shock and horror.

The inquiry was born of panic over false claims that the *News of the World* deleted Milly Dowler's emails and that the *Sun* blagged medical records on Gordon Brown's child. Those allegations killed the *News of the World*, cost 300 jobs and triggered a marathon probe that has roamed to the outer limits of its original terms of reference.

The Leveson Inquiry invited anyone with a grievance to vent their spleen, on oath but without cross-examination or protection against hearsay evidence or leading questions. Yet it has the potential to curb free speech, shackle a free press and inhibit the right to examine the conduct of those who rule over us.

The inquiry was, it must be said, entitled to examine unacceptable and sometimes illegal practices by some journalists on most newspapers. Yet no apology (of which there have been many), no level of compensation (many millions) and no retribution (dawn police raids, criminal charges and the *NoW* closure itself) is enough to assuage the indignation of those for whom this investigation has been poetic justice.

Lord Justice Leveson says he does not intend his conclusions to end up as a 'footnote' in some professor of journalism's memoirs. So what can we expect?

His lordship does not like tabloids – even if millions do. His inquiry has sometimes strayed into the realm of political correctness – Page Three girls, the coverage of Islamism and even jokes about speech impediments.

Even as I write this, I wonder if he might haul me in to explain myself. That is the effect of the Leveson Inquiry. Newspaper editors who might normally rage about free speech have gone mute, perhaps to avoid retribution.

So it was left to Education Secretary Michael Gove to defend Fleet Street. He upset the judge by noting 'a chilling atmosphere towards freedom of expression which emanates from the debate around Leveson'. 'Free speech doesn't mean anything unless some people are going to be offended some of the time', he said. A statement of the blindingly obvious, you might think.

But not to a worryingly thin-skinned Lord Leveson, who complained to Downing Street and threatened to resign. He did so in private and was even angrier when it was splashed all over the *Mail on Sunday*. His knee-jerk response was to carpet the editor. He was talked out of that, but the fact that it even crossed his mind should make every journalist uneasy.

Lord Leveson insists he has no 'hidden agenda', did not try to gag Gove and believes the press is entitled to say what it likes. But he believes the story was published at his expense to defend Fleet Street's interests. The fact that it was in the PUBLIC interest seems to have passed him by.

So what should Lord Leveson do? Preferably as little as possible.

We do not need to be licensed like dogs and gun owners. Nor a professional body like the General Medical Council or the Law Society, neither of which have covered themselves in glory. Prior disclosure is the kiss of death for important stories.

But 'something' must be done.

So what about a beefed-up complaints procedure, a new, more robust version of the PCC with an ombudsman offering free conciliation? It could compel a newspaper to print an apology, retraction or correction – in extreme cases on Page One. But we should think twice about cash awards which would expose all newspapers, national and local, to the no-win, no-fee vultures.

In America, under the First Amendment, citizens are free to say what they like, even if it offends – except shouting 'fire' in a crowded theatre. In Europe, privacy laws allow the rich and powerful to conceal corruption – and they are spreading here like noxious weeds.

Judging by Lord Justice Leveson's response to his own experience of an investigative press, he leans towards the European system. If so, it won't be his legacy that is consigned to a footnote. It will be the hard-won, centuries-old and almost irreplaceable tradition of a truly free press.

Trevor Kavanagh is the *Sun*'s associate editor

Powerful institutions, including media organisations, are not in the business of self-expression, and should not go into that business. An argument that speech should be free because it generally does not affect, *a fortiori* can't harm, others can't stretch to cover the speech of governments or large corporations, of News International or the BBC.

Big media corporations have voices far louder than individuals or small publishers. They are watched, listened to and read by millions. Their capacity to do harm is disproportionately greater for this reason. They are also able to drown out smaller voices, to deprive individuals and groups of the opportunity to speak for themselves. And, should someone try to get some redress if they have been 'monstered', demonised or unjustifiably intruded upon, the corporation has the legal firepower to prevent all but the richest and most powerful from taking action.

Reforms should, for this reason, focus on these large corporations. Individuals, bloggers, tweeters, independent news sites, small magazines and newspapers should not be Leveson's focus. They should be free to publish whatever they like within the law. They should be excluded from any regulatory obligations that might risk constraining their free speech.

Large corporations should still be free to publish what they like – they have a right to free speech too – but require a regulatory obligation to take responsibility for what they publish. In other words, they should have the mechanisms in place to justify their decisions to intrude on someone's privacy. Equally, they should provide a decent opportunity for the subject of a story to respond, ensuring a fair hearing and potentially fair redress if an individual believes what was written to be misrepresentative or inaccurate. These accountability mechanisms should be both internal and external.

In the 60 years before the Leveson Inquiry was set up, there were three Royal Commissions on the Press, two inquiries into privacy, and countless calls for press reform. All were pleas for powerful press barons to take some responsibility. Each time these large organisations failed to respond adequately.

Lord Justice Leveson says he does not want his recommendations to gather dust on some academic's shelf. Nor does he want his inquiry succeeded by yet another in a decade's time. If that is the case, then he should focus reforms on big media organisations and oblige them, for the first time, to take proper responsibility for what they do.

Martin Moore is director of the Media Standards Trust and a founder of the Hacked Off campaign. The Media Standards Trust report, *A Free and Accountable Media*, can be found at www.mediastandardstrust.org

A new settlement by Alan Rusbridger

I have always believed that the most interesting period in the phone hacking story was the 18-month period following the *Guardian*'s original revelation of the Gordon Taylor settlement – which blew apart News International's 'one rotten apple' defence in July 2009. It was interesting precisely because almost nothing happened. All the dogs one would expect to bark in such a situation stayed silent. From the politicians, to the police, to the regulator, to the press themselves.

The Leveson Inquiry has finally given us some insight into what was happening in this period. The inquiry has had criticism – some merited, some not. But no one can doubt that Leveson has uncovered uncomfortable truths about the way a number of journalists – as well as politicians and police – have worked in the past. In what other sphere of public life do we think that transparency of this kind is an undesirable thing? I am confident that good things can flow from holding the press up to scrutiny, however difficult it may have been at times.

The press in this country has been under-regulated but over-legislated. There is a risk that by addressing only one side of this equation – by only strengthening regulation – the inquiry will undermine the strength of our press to do the work we all deem so vital. We therefore argued the inquiry should redress the balance between regulation and legislation and make recommendations that meet the twin objectives of protecting the public and protecting press freedom. It is not possible to improve the culture, practice and ethics of the press without protecting and promoting the best of journalism in the public interest. We believe therefore in a new settlement which will address four deficiencies.

Defamation

The 2011 Global Press Freedom Rankings placed the UK in joint 26th place. Libel law has been cited by many investigative journalists as the main constraint on their work. The current defamation bill makes some improvements but says little, for example, on early dispute resolution. Libel is an essential piece of this jigsaw, especially through an alternative dispute resolution system which we hope Lord Justice Leveson will propose.

Plurality

Another measure of freedom is whether reporters are genuinely free to follow any story they wish – or to what extent proprietorial, editorial or commercial pressures circumscribe, or otherwise influence, the freedom to report on matters of genuine public interest. Without the sort of plurality that enables the *Guardian* to exist as well as other, much bigger and wealthier titles, it's doubtful we would have learned about phone hacking. It is understandable that Leveson does not feel able to do a full review of plurality jurisprudence. But anything which concentrates power in the hands of fewer and fewer multi-billionaire proprietors will impoverish our society. The current plurality framework – which apparently granted no one the power to intervene over the BSkyB deal – is plainly insufficient to ensure the kind of plurality that is necessary for a healthy democracy. And this is about more than News Corporation, as anyone following developments in Australian media ownership will testify.

Public interest journalism under threat

While the digital transition brings many benefits – above all, an explosion in free expression that enriches democratic discourse – we must tackle one of its less desirable consequences: a diminution in public interest journalism. Investigative journalism – costly, unpredictable and with no direct revenues attached – is often among the first savings to be made. Other forms of reporting – foreign correspondents, court reporters, specialists – are next. So editors and reporters simply don't have the freedom to do the reporting that society may want or need. Regulation should therefore enhance the climate for this work, not diminish it. This will include protections for public interest journalism in regulation as well as through consistent application of public interest defences in laws affecting the media.

Regulation

The press must accept that the breach of trust engendered by a series of Editors' Code breaches and a discredited PCC needs tackling immediately and resolutely. That's why we have argued for an ambitious system of regulation that includes the use of an alternative dispute resolution system that benefits both complainants and publishers by delivering meaningful redress for breaches of the Editors' Code, quickly and cheaply. A measure of this strength is essential to prevent the introduction of compulsory or statutory mechanisms to deliver full participation that may undermine press freedom. But it also demonstrates that the press is determined to improve its standards and practices without recourse to judges.

So let's hope that Leveson proposes a balanced package of proposals, in effect a new settlement that both restores trust in journalism and strengthens our role in serving the public interest.

Alan Rusbridger is editor-in chief, Guardian News & Media

Do we need a free press? by Mark Lewis

Time and again, the criticism of the Leveson Inquiry is that it is another nail in the coffin of a free press. Who says so? The press themselves. Who are they kidding?

My answer to anyone who raises this argument to me is: 'How sweet, you really believe that we have a free press!' Stop and look at the phone-hacking scandal. Not the actions of those involved (one scandal), but all those newspapers that did not even report the story (another scandal). Post-Dowler, *The Times* ran an editorial apologising for not telling its readers. So many papers misled their readership by saying nothing. Absolute censorship. It does not suit us for our readers to know, so we will not tell them. Censorship backed up by the non-regulatory regulator: the Press Complaints Commission. We want it to stay and regulate us, say the press. It isn't a regulator says the PCC's new chairman, Lord Hunt. So there you have it, demands by the press for the preservation of non-regulation. A licence to print anything, a licence to ruin lives and, more sinister, a licence to cover up. Which journalist feels able to write an article that accuses his editor? That's a problem Lord Justice Leveson won't be addressing

No matter how strong an advocate one is of freedom of speech, it does not equate with an unrestricted freedom of the press. It is often lost (although not on LJ Leveson) that 'free speech' and a 'free press' are not interchangeable concepts. Test the theory: a paedophile wishes to sell pornographic pictures of children. Should he be prevented from doing so? Of course. I doubt anyone would argue seriously that such abuse should be aggravated just because of freedom. I suspect the ubiquitous tabloid reader would (rightly) express moral outrage. Ironically, the same reader who would argue that we should stop that publication would baulk at the idea of any form of censorship.

So let's see where we draw the line. We do need some form of censorship, even John Kampfner, former chief executive of *Index on Censorship*, would agree. There are times when the balance drops on the side of preventing publication. The press seems to be obsessed with exposing adulterous affairs of footballers and the medical treatment of celebrities, but is not keen at all on any issues regarding journalists. When did you last read of adultery by an editor? Speeding by a journalist? Or drug taking by an opinion writer? Are these the most moral, sober, narcotic-free role models? Or is it that the freedoms they cherish so much include the freedom not to write anything harmful about themselves or their colleagues.

We need to move away from hypocritical attempts to defend scurrilous story-writing by the sanctimonious utterances of those who should know better. The freedoms we want are not freedoms to ruin lives, to gossip or to distract. That is not the free press we strive for: what we want is the freedom to write on any subject about anyone within the confines of good taste. We do not want to have a press that is controlled by a state, but we also do not want to have a press controlled by a quasi-state such as a large corporation.

Leveson has put the ethics of the press in the spotlight. The relationship with the Metropolitan Police has been exposed. People must still ask why a crime was not investigated while the reviewer of that case, John Yates (who described his six-hour review as a 'bit crap'), did not re-open a case that subsequently led to Operations Weeting and Elveden. We know from Leveson that the *News of the World* thought it was entitled to a payback for the glasses of champagne that it had bought for Yates.

The biggest lesson that we have learnt from the inquiry so far is that we have a press-controlled state rather than a state-controlled press. As Rupert Murdoch made clear, he never asked a prime minister for anything. Surely, the response should be: 'Exactly, everyone else has to ask.'

Will Leveson deliver? I hope so. The issue is far more wide-reaching than the alleged criminal activities of a few, or even the ability to determine a complaints mechanism that avoids the 'chilling effect' of disproportionately expensive legal cases – it concerns democracy itself. We need politicians who are able to represent the people even if our interests are opposed to those of the press; we need police who act against the press without fear of reprisals, and we need journalists who are prepared to tell us what their bosses don't want us to read.

Mark Lewis is a partner at Taylor Hampton. He represents many clients whose privacy was invaded by the News of the World. He also acted for Dr Peter Wilmshurst and the Sheffield Wednesday fans who were sued for libel

© Marta Cooper, Trevor Kavanagh, Guido Fawkes, Mark Lewis, Martin Moore and Alan Rusbridger
41(3): 14/26
DOI: 10.1177/0306422012457320
www.indexoncensorship.org

Clinically proven to rebuild skin cells

Benefits of wheatgrass juice

Sleep on the left to avoid stillbirth

Shun the obscure chemicals

GM trial vandalised

MRSA resistant pyjamas

Head massage in schools

Olive oil cuts risk of stroke by 41%

modulates the harmful effects of electromagnetic radiation

Optimise the release of energy from our diet

Can goats' blood help beat MS?

Scientist silenced by libel threat

Everybody needs to talk about evidence

Everybody can question claims about risks or benefits – on websites, products, adverts, guidelines, publications or policy announcements – and ask for the evidence.
If more consumers, patients and voters ask for the evidence, those making claims will expect to be held to account.

Ask for evidence is supported by leading scientists, entertainers and community leaders, and many scientific and civic groups. Join the campaign, gets hints and tips on asking for evidence and read stories and advice from other people who have done this at www.senseaboutscience.org/a4e

Sense About Science is a charity that helps people to make sense of science and evidence. We stand up for scientific debate, free from stigma, intimidation, hysteria or censorship. And we encourage everyone, whatever their experience, to insist on evidence in public life.

sense about science

www.senseaboutscience.org
Registered Charity No. 1146170, Company No. 6771027

@senseaboutsci #askforevidence

THE GEEK EFFECT

As UK campaigners make the last push for libel reform, **Mark Henderson** considers the unexpected impact of a new force in activism

At 7pm on 18 May 2009, about 300 people packed into the basement of the Penderel's Oak pub in Holborn for a public meeting. Professor Brian Cox, the physicist, broadcaster and former pop star, was among the speakers, and so was Dave Gorman, the comedian, but the main draw was a less well-known name – an excitable science writer with John Lennon glasses and a spiky haircut.

The assembly of assorted sceptics, bloggers and scientists had come to listen to Simon Singh, the author of *Big Bang* and *Fermat's Last Theorem*. He wasn't there because he had a new book to promote. He was there because he was fighting a libel case that could easily bankrupt him.

Just over a year before the meeting, Singh had marked Chiropractic Awareness Week by raising a little awareness of the alternative therapy in the pages of the *Guardian*. 'You might think that modern chiropractors restrict themselves to treating back problems,' he wrote, 'but in fact they still possess some quite wacky ideas. The British Chiropractic Association (BCA) claims that their members can help treat children with colic, sleeping and feeding problems, frequent ear infections, asthma and prolonged crying, even though there is not a jot of evidence. This organisation is the respectable face of the chiropractic profession and yet it happily promotes bogus treatments.'

The respectable face of the chiropractic profession did not seek to rebut the charge with evidence. Instead, the chiropractors sued for libel – with every prospect of victory.

England's defamation laws are notoriously friendly to claimants, who need not show that an alleged libel is false. The burden of proof lies on the defendant, who must demonstrate his assertion to be true, or a matter of fair comment. The legal costs involved are so steep, often running to hundreds of thousands of pounds, that even defendants who are sure of their facts can be cowed into submission for fear of bankruptcy.

With the financial resources to sue, the BCA saw an opportunity to force one of Britain's most vocal and effective critics of alternative medicine to eat his words. And when the geeks gathered at Penderel's Oak, that seemed a very real possibility. A few days beforehand, Mr Justice Eady had ruled that by using the word 'bogus', Singh had implied deliberate dishonesty on behalf of the British Chiropractic Association – a charge he never intended, and which would be exceptionally difficult to defend. He was on the point of giving in.

The chiropractors, however, had reckoned without the geeks. And their intervention in support of Singh was not only to turn the course of his case but to catalyse a campaign for libel law reform that, three years on, is starting to bear fruit.

The BCA's oversight was perfectly understandable. People with a passion for science, and the critical thinking on which it is founded, have never been particularly conspicuous in public life, let alone formed a constituency to be crossed at your peril. Yet something has been stirring among the geeks. Drawn together by the social networking power of the internet, they've stopped apologising for their interests, and are beginning to become a force in politics and society.

Through vibrant blogs and online forums such as Twitter and Facebook, and through the success of increasingly high-profile figures such as Singh, Cox and Ben Goldacre, geeks and sceptics are starting to fight for the value of science and evidence-based thinking.

The geeks are on the march. The BCA foolishly threw itself in the way.

Even before the chiropractors decided to mess with Simon Singh, many geeks had become dogged pursuers of homeopaths, anti-vaccine activists, dodgy nutritionists and other purveyors of quackery and pseudoscience.

Some geeks are scientists. Some are doctors. Many are neither. All, though, care deeply about the scientific method: the most reliable tool humanity has yet developed for distinguishing truth from falsehood. 'We're rationalists,' as Singh puts it. 'We aren't necessarily scientists, but we have an affinity for science.'

Geeks take a forensic approach to the evidence behind medical claims, and are strongly committed to unfettered debate. The chiropractors' writ could scarcely have been better calculated to rile them. Legal bullying was shutting down rational argument. No self-respecting geek was going to stand for it.

As news of the law suit reached the blogosphere, geeks bearing noms de plume such as Gimpy and Zeno, the Quackometer and Adventures in Nonsense rallied to Singh's support. Almost 10,000 people joined a Facebook group started by David Allen Green, a lawyer who blogs as Jack of Kent. Others weighed in on Twitter. Many offered money to finance the defence, which Singh declined. As a bestselling author, he had the means to fight. The question was whether he had the stomach for a legal battle that might effectively become a full-time job for years on end.

That stomach was never more sorely tested than in the days after Eady's 'bogus ruling'. Yet as he weighed up whether or not to settle and apologise, the groundswell of support he received both in person at Penderel's Oak and from many more well-wishers online steeled his nerve.

'The reaction was extraordinary,' Singh says. 'There was a point in May when I was close to caving in. That support was really important. It made me think: "Simon, you're not crazy. You're not the only one who thinks this matters."'

Green agrees that the geeks were crucial. 'No one would have thought badly of Simon if he had just brought the case to a halt,' he wrote later on his blog. 'The ever-growing online support helped keep him soldiering on.'

It wasn't just moral support that was on offer from these welcome allies. A devastating counter-attack was soon under way. When the BCA released what it called a 'plethora of evidence' supporting chiropractic as an effective treatment for childhood ailments such as colic and asthma, a battalion of bloggers demolished every claim within 24 hours. If the claimant were to rely on this in court, the defence would have refutations to hand.

Then there was what Green dubbed the 'quacklash'. Unlike most other alternative therapists, such as homeopaths or reflexologists, chiropractors are regulated in the UK. They must adhere to a set of professional guidelines that include obtaining informed consent from their patients, and they are subject to trading and advertising standards, which do not allow claims that are not supported by evidence.

Bloggers such as Andy Lewis (the Quackometer), Simon Perry (Adventures in Nonsense) and Alan Henness (Zeno's Blog) began to trawl chiropractors' websites for misleading and unsupported medical assertions. They then reported those who appeared to be in breach of regulatory standards. 'I don't think there could be a better use of £75 worth of stamps,' wrote Perry.

There was no shortage of suitable targets. In June 2009, shortly after Mr Justice Eady's preliminary ruling, the General Chiropractic Council received complaints about more than 500 individual practitioners in the space of one day. Chiropractors went into full-blown damage-limitation mode. Lewis got hold of an email from the McTimoney Chiropractic Association urging its members to take down their websites and 'to remove any patient information leaflets of your own that state you treat whiplash, colic or other childhood problems in your clinic'. These, of course, were the very claims Singh had questioned to prompt the BCA's writ.

By resorting to law, the back-crackers inflicted terrible self-harm. In trying to silence a critic, the BCA invited unprecedented scrutiny of the evidence base for its techniques. Newspapers that hadn't covered the original lawsuit gleefully reported the quacklash and the threat to free speech. There was suddenly a news hook for articles examining the questionable claims made for chiropractic, and the Kafkaesque anachronisms of English libel law.

Even were the BCA to win at trial, damage to the reputation it sued to protect would reach a different scale to anything inflicted by Singh's original column. But the victory was to be Singh's. In April 2010, the court of appeal overturned Mr Justice Eady's ruling in a withering judgment, and the chiropractors dropped their case. Singh's supporters celebrated on their blogs and on Twitter by posting: 'The BCA happily promotes bogus treatments.' One in four British chiropractors was under investigation by regulators at the time.

Geek activism had helped Singh to win a seminal case, which established an important legal precedent that should protect other scientists and writers. 'Scientific controversies must be settled by the methods of science rather than by the methods of litigation,' the judgment noted. But the campaign achieved something else besides, focusing public attention on the chilling effect of English libel law on public discourse.

The libel action turned Singh – well known for a science writer but hardly a household name – into a cause célèbre. He became a symbol of free speech and principled scepticism, championed by celebrities such as Ricky Gervais, Dara Ó Briain and Stephen Fry. But the movement didn't stop there.

Science writer Simon Singh (second left) with supporters outside the High Court, London in 2010,
after he won his libel battle against the British Chiropractic Association (BCA)
Credit: Fiona Hanson/PA

Galvanised by the Penderel's Oak meeting, Tracey Brown and Sile Lane, of the charity Sense About Science, began a 'Keep Libel Laws Out of Science' petition, soon to carry 20,000 names. They then joined forces with Index on Censorship and English PEN, to begin a wider campaign for libel reform that rapidly began to gather pace.

The narrow aversion of a serious injustice, which still left a vindicated Singh £60,000 out of pocket because of legal costs he could not recover, offered convincing evidence that libel law had become a serious threat to free expression. It was even a threat to public health: if medical techniques and technologies could not be criticised without risking a defamation suit, they could not receive the scrutiny that is necessary to protect patients.

This was a message that campaigners could take to MPs with every chance of convincing them, not least because the Singh case was no isolated incident. Peter Wilmshurst, a British cardiologist, found himself defending a libel action after he criticised a heart device made by an American company. His remarks were made at a conference in the United States, and reported by a North American website, but the writ was filed in London. He faced bankruptcy and the loss of his home.

Cases such as Singh's and Wilmshurst's offered clear evidence that libel reform was not simply an obsession of tabloid journalists still smarting over the award of million-pound damages to celebrities like Elton John. Defamation was being used to stifle the kind of criticism without which science cannot properly take place.

This was a message that was sufficient to convince Labour, the Liberal Democrats and the Conservatives to support reform in their 2010 election manifestos. And on 9 May 2012, a Defamation Bill was included in the Queen's Speech.

This bill is imperfect, but it does offer an opportunity to begin to reform a libel system about which journalists, human rights activists and some lawyers had been complaining for years, with little effect.

Through the Singh case, geeks provided a catalyst for change. They made it plain that the cause of libel reform was not simply a sectional interest of a media that wanted to peddle poorly sourced gossip without fear of sanction. When legitimate scientific criticism of medical interventions stood at risk of being silenced, libel became a matter of public interest and public health.

Through their outspoken activism in support of Singh, and Wilmshurst, the geeks succeeded in forcing libel reform onto the political agenda where others had failed. Their message was one that resonated with MPs, many of whom were prepared to stick up for the unfettered discourse of science when they would have been reluctant to defend the perceived interests of the *Sun* and the *News of the World*.

Geeks turned libel reform into a cause that reasonable politicians could no longer ignore. And as the Defamation Bill begins its final journey to the statute book, they are again at the forefront of efforts to improve it with remorseless lobbying to ensure that no one speaking out in the public interest can be silenced or bullied. ❐

©Mark Henderson
41(3): 28/34
DOI: 10.1177/0306422012456136
www.indexoncensorship.org

Mark Henderson is the author of *The Geek Manifesto: Why Science Matters* (Bantam Press)

International Books of
Passion and Power

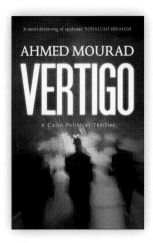

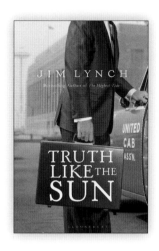

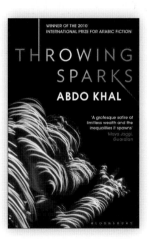

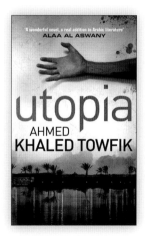

دار بلومزبري – مؤسسة قطر للنشر
BLOOMSBURY
QATAR FOUNDATION
PUBLISHING

مؤسسة قطر
Qatar Foundation

BLOOMSBURY

www.bloomsbury.com · www.bqfp.com.qa

HAROLD PINTER

Blowing up the media

American Football
(a reflection upon the Gulf War)

Hallelujah!
It works.
We blew the shit out of them.

We blew the shit right back up their
own ass

It works.
We blew the shit out of them.
They suffocated in their own shit!

Hallelujah.
Praise the Lord for all good things.

We blew them into fucking shit.
They are eating it.

Praise the Lord for all good things.

We blew their balls into shards of dust,
Into shards of fucking dust.

We did it.

Now I want you to come over here and
kiss me on the mouth.

Harold Pinter
August 1991

I started to write this poem on the plane
going to the Edinburgh Festival in August
1991. I had a rough draft by the time we
landed in Edinburgh. It sprang from the
triumphalism, the *machismo*, the victory
parades, that were very much in evidence at
the time. So that is the reason for 'We blew
the shit out of them.' The first place I sent it to
was the *London Review of Books*. I received a
very odd letter, which said, in sum, that the
poem had considerable force, but it was for
that very reason that they were not able to
publish it. But the letter went on to make the
extraordinary assertion that the paper shared
my views about the USA's role in the world.
So I wrote back. The paper shares my views,

behind you myself, speaking personally.' This
is my memory of the telephone conversation.
'But,' he said, 'you know I don't think …
Oooh, I think we're in for real trouble if we
try to publish it in the *Guardian*.' Really, I
asked innocently, why is that?

He said, 'Well, you know, Harold, we are
a family newspaper.' Those words were
actually said. 'Oh, I'm sorry,' I said, 'I was
under the impression you were a serious
newspaper.' And he said, 'Well, yes, we're
also a serious newspaper, of course.
Nevertheless things have changed a bit in the
Guardian over the last few years.'

I suggested he talk to some of his colleagues
and come back to me in a couple of days.
Because, I said, 'I do believe the *Guardian*
has a responsibility to publish serious work,
seriously considered work, which I believe
this to be. Although it is very hot, I also
think it is steely. Hot steel …'

He called me in two days and said, 'Harold,
I'm terribly sorry, I can't publish it.' He
more or less said, It's more than my job's
worth. So that was the *Guardian*. I then sent
it to the *Observer* …

Which has published your poems previously …

Oh yes, the *Guardian* has published me in
the past, too … As, incidentally, has the
Independent. The *Observer* was the most
complex and fascinating web that I actually
ran into. I sent the poem not to the literary
editor, but to the editor himself.

A couple of days later, he called me and
said that he thought it should be published.
He thought it was very testing. Probably
going to be quite a lot of flack, he said. But
he thought it should be published, not on the
literary pages, but on the leader page. It was
a truly political poem, he said. So I was
delighted to hear that. He'd send me a proof,
which he did.

The next Sunday nothing happened. And
then the following Sunday nothing happened.
So I called the editor. He said, 'Oh dear,
Harold, I'm afraid that I've run into one or
two problems with your poem.' I asked what
they were. 'So short, the substance was. And
want me to publish it … why not the said.

'They're telling me …
of readers …
their …
He said …

GULF STORM

Harold Pinter talked to *Index*'s editor about the poem that no one wanted to publish, written in response to the war against Iraq in 1991

Harold Pinter: I started to write this poem on the plane going to the Edinburgh Festival in August 1991. I had a rough draft by the time we landed in Edinburgh. It sprang from the triumphalism, the machismo, the victory parades, that were very much in evidence at the time. So that is the reason for 'We blew the shit out of them'. The first place I sent it to was the *London Review of Books*. I received a very odd letter, which said, in sum, that the poem had considerable force, but it was for that very reason that they were not able to publish it. But the letter went on to make the extraordinary assertion that the paper shared my views about the USA's role in the world. So I wrote back. 'The paper shares my views, does it? I'd keep that to myself if I were you, chum,' I said. And I was very pleased with the use of the word 'chum'.

So I sent it to the *Guardian* and the then literary editor came on the telephone to me and said, 'Oh dear.' He said, 'Harold, this is really… You've really given me a very bad headache with this one.' He said, 'I'm entirely behind you myself, speaking personally.' This is my memory of the telephone conversation. 'But,' he said, 'you know I don't think … Oooh, I think we're in for real trouble if we try to publish it in the *Guardian*.' Really, I asked innocently, why is that?

He said, 'Well, you know, Harold, we are a family newspaper.' Those words were actually said. 'Oh, I'm sorry,' I said, 'I was under the impression you were a serious newspaper.' And he said, 'Well, yes, we're also a serious newspaper, of course. Nevertheless things have changed a bit in the *Guardian* over the last few years.'

I suggested he talk to some of his colleagues and come back to me in a couple of days. Because, I said, 'I do believe the *Guardian* has a responsibility to publish serious work, seriously considered work, which I believe this to be. Although it is very hot, I also think it is steely. Hot steel…'

He called me in two days and said, 'Harold, I'm terribly sorry, I can't publish it.' He more or less said, It's more than my job's worth. So that was the *Guardian*. I then sent it to the *Observer*…

Andrew Graham-Yooll: Which has published your poems previously…

Oh yes, the *Guardian* has published me in the past, too … As, incidentally, has the *Independent*. The *Observer* was the most complex and fascinating web that I actually ran into. I sent the poem not to the literary editor, but to the editor himself.

A couple of days later, he called me and said that he thought it should be published. He thought it was very testing. Probably going to be quite a lot of flack, he said. But he thought it should be published, not on the literary pages, but on the leader page. It was a truly political poem, he said. So I was delighted to hear that. He'd send me a proof, which he did.

The next Sunday nothing happened. And then the following Sunday nothing happened. So I called the editor. He said, 'Oh dear, Harold, I'm afraid that I've run into one or two problems with your poem.' I asked what they were. 'In short, my colleagues don't want me to publish it.' Why not? He said, 'They're telling me we are going to lose lots of readers.' I asked, Do you really believe that? Anyway, we had a quite amiable chat. He said, 'I want to publish it but I seem to be more or less alone.' I then said, look, the *Observer*, as a serious newspaper, has in fact published quite recently an account of what the US tanks actually did in the desert. The tanks had bulldozers, and during the ground attack they were used as sweepers. They buried, as far as we know, an untold number of Iraqis alive. This was reported by your newspaper as a fact and it was a horrific and obscene fact. My poem actually says, 'They suffocated in their own shit.' It is obscene, but it is referring to obscene facts.

He said, 'Absolutely right. Look, I want to publish the poem. But I'm running into all sorts of resistance. The trouble is the language, it's the obscene language. People get very offended by this and that's why they think we are going to lose readers.' I then sent the editor of the *Observer* a short fax, in which I quoted myself when I was at the US Embassy in Ankara in March 1985 with Arthur Miller. I had a chat with the ambassador about torture in Turkish prisons. He told me that I didn't appreciate the realities of the situation vis-à-vis the communist threat, the military reality, the diplomatic reality, the strategic reality, and so on.

I said the reality I was referring to was that of electric current on your genitals. Whereupon the ambassador said, 'Sir, you are a guest in my house,' and turned away. I left the house.

The point I was making to the editor of the *Observer* was that the ambassador found great offence in the word genitals. But the reality of the situation, the actual reality of electric current on your genitals, was a matter of no concern to him. It was the use of the *word* that was offensive, but not the act. I said I was drawing an analogy between that little exchange, and what we were now talking about. This poem uses obscene words to describe obscene acts and obscene attitudes.

But the editor of the *Observer* wrote to me and said he couldn't publish, with great regret. 'I've been giving serious thought to publication of your poem on the Gulf War. As you know, my first instinct was in favour, despite warnings by senior colleagues that many readers would be offended … I admit to having cold feet.' Recently an *Observer* columnist spoke of his paper's rejection of the poem and referred to his editor's concern 'for its shortcomings as a piece of verse'. This was not of course true. The editor showed no such concern – to me, at least.

I then sent the poem to the literary editor of the *Independent*, saying I hadn't sent it to him in the first place because I did not think the *Independent* would publish it. But now that everybody had turned it down, the *London Review of Books*, the *Guardian* and the *Observer*, perhaps I was wrong about the *Independent*! To cut a long story very short, the literary editor wanted to publish it but he felt he had to show it to the editor. The editor sat on it for a few days and then made no comment except to say the *Independent* was not going to publish the poem. And I've never had any explanation. Nothing. It was simply no.

The *London Review of Books'* letter was dated 24 September 1991; the *Guardian's* rejection came in a conversation on the telephone at the beginning of October. The letter from the editor of the Observer was dated 6 November, and that from the *Independent* was dated 9 December.

In conversation earlier, you said you would rather not write down the record of this poem yourself, because it would sound as if you were whingeing. But there is an issue here beyond the complaint of the rejected poet. This poem has been dropped by the mainstream press, which would normally have snapped up anything written by Harold Pinter.

I did, incidentally, send it to the *New York Review of Books*, just as a laugh. The editor thanked me warmly for sending the poem, but said he was afraid they couldn't use it. So I finally did not waste any more time. I heard that a magazine called *Bomb,* a very well produced publication in the West Village, might be interested, and indeed they published the poem.

It was also finally published in Britain, in January 1992, by a new newspaper called *Socialist*, with a limited circulation. But as far as national newspapers go, in Holland it was published in one of the main Dutch dailies, *Handelsblad* – in no uncertain terms, too, with an article about the rejection in England, written by the editor. And it was published in Bulgaria, Greece and Finland.

It is interesting, isn't it? At a time when papers are not too troubled about the severity of thelanguage, when it is about the body, scatological, sexual, or whatever. We have overcome

the years when you had to put a series of dots in place of an 'F' word. Yet the objection to
your poem was justified in your use of some strong words.

This may be because it is a formed piece of work, and perhaps that is where its strength lies. It is a deliberate piece of work. So it alarms more. I'd like to say, as the poet, that I regard it as a very ugly poem. It is necessarily ugly. Its reference is to the grossest ugliness.

But nobody ever said, 'We don't think this poem is good enough. It is not a successful piece of work.' Nobody has actually said that.

I feel particularly sensitive about the language. I am the editor of Index on Censorship
responsible for losing Index an annual grant of £7,000. Somebody objected to the word
'cunt'in an article in our special issue on women, Breaking the silence (9/1990).
I thought the word, though strong, was in context. However, although I do not know the
exact details, one funding organisation obviously took exception. I wonder what would
happen if your poem were to be re-submitted now, as an exercise.People and editors
change, and their opinions and reactions change. Perhaps it would be an exercise worth
pursuing … The reactions seem to be so final for the wrong reasons: 'family paper', or
'offending readers'…

Oh no. I have no intention of re-submitting it – or anything else – to any of these newspapers. Unless I decide to write nursery rhymes.

At a time when we have become far more accustomed to strong language in print, it is
almost amusing to find sensitivities expressed in this way. Perhaps it reflects this very
peculiar political period we are living in. There is a rather coy and false reaction to matters
and events, which are 'strong' in themselves. Brutal language is shunned as a way of
avoiding brutal issues.

I think that is a valid conclusion to be drawn. It was well known and has been often asserted that the sanitisation of the Gulf War was palpable. The actual nature of the horror was hardly ever aired, or seen on TV. Such a thing as this poem, for me, is about opening a curtain which many people would prefer to see remain closed. And it is in the interests of government that that curtain,that veil, is forever drawn over the nature of reality.

Every war has its share of blood and dripping guts, and bodies blown to pieces, but barring
one photo published by the Observer, as it happens, of a carbonised figure above a tank,
this war had no dripping guts.

None of it then, and none of it wanted as a reminder now. You can trace the history of the present state of affairs to a series of events through the 1980s, which I am quite clear about. I'm talking of the US invasion of Grenada in 1983, the 'low intensity' war against Nicaragua, the invasion of Panama in 1989, followed by the Gulf War. I do believe this is what I represent in the last line of the poem: 'Now I want you to come over here and kiss me on the mouth.' It refers to who is the boss, who is in charge, who is the master.

But the behaviour of the media is crucial in all this. It has been confirmed that the number of deaths in Panama approached 4,000. But at the time the media talked in hundreds.

Do you remember the revolution in Romania in 1989? The TV was full of statements saying 80,000 people had been killed, especially around Timisoara. The true figure, as I understand it, is about 1,000.

So we are really talking about a controlled media. What the western media actually does is blow up or exaggerate certain facts in its own interests – or in its government's interests – and ignore and suppress other facts. The dead in Iraq and the continuing deaths in Iraq are hardly front-page news. ❐

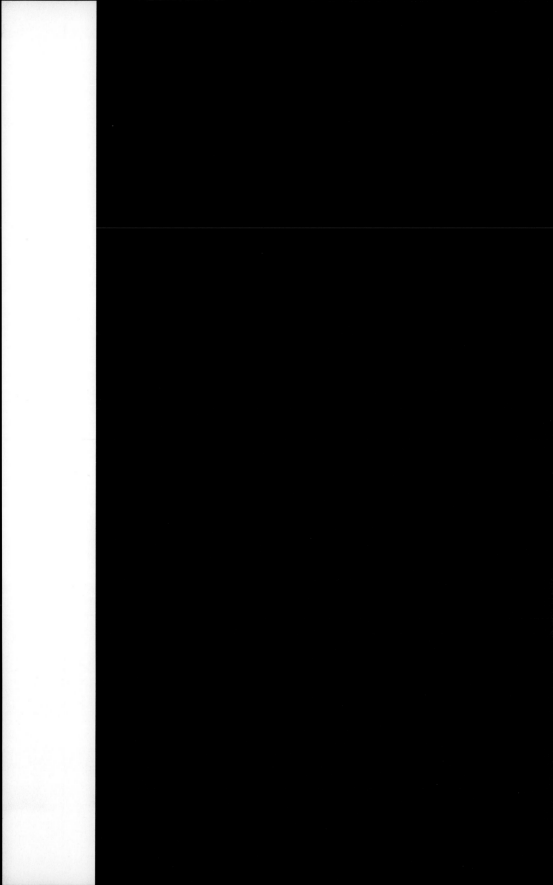

CENSORS ON CAMPUS

The global chill on academic freedom:
from the UK to Thailand

Academics, activists, students and civilians march against anti-monarchy laws that stifle free speech, 14 February 2012, Bangkok, Thailand
Credit: Lillian Suwanrumpha/Demotix/Demotix/Press Association Images

RESEARCH BY NUMBERS

Academic freedom is in danger. **Thomas Docherty** explains how cuts are hijacking the pursuit of knowledge in the UK's universities

One morning in June 1946, Hannah Arendt received a package at her home in New York. As a Jew, Arendt had not been permitted to teach in German universities; and, like many German-Jewish intellectuals, she found refuge in America. The package she received that morning contained a book, *The Idea of the University*, written by her former academic supervisor, Karl Jaspers. It was a new edition of a book Jaspers had initially published in 1923; in its 1946 revision, it became a contribution to the de-Nazification of the German university system and German society. Arendt read it avidly, immediately exploring the possibility of having it translated for a wide audience.

The book was amongst the first to formulate a post-war credo of academic freedom. Jaspers saw its importance for the renewed health of a university system and of a society that had been corrupted by authoritarian restrictions on freedom of thought, speech and action under Nazism. Academic freedom permits the scholar to follow fearlessly whatever lines of inquiry are demanded by the disinterested pursuit of truth and knowledge in any field; and the actual and material realisation of this freedom lies in the dissemination of such knowledge through teaching. To teach is to enact those very freedoms of thought that academic research strives to imagine.

Substantial funding cuts in the UK are severely undermining Jasper's tenets. Since Lord Browne's higher education review two years ago recommended slashing the university teaching budget by 80 per cent, the pace has accelerated. In a climate of public sector austerity there now even appears to be a logic to the cuts, but the impact on academic freedom is profound. Why does it matter? The licence to engage with ideas that are critical of social norms and existing values depends on that freedom. Its curtailment encourages the establishment of orthodoxy and promotes authoritarian forms of governance that stifle freely spoken critique.

The 1946 context makes clear what is at stake: the university, built on academic freedom, is an institution that seeks to realise the freedoms that will give an emergent democratic society its various identities, arguments, and openness to future possibilities. Such openness of spirit had been precluded while the university sector was the instrument of an ideologically determined political programme. Nazism permitted only those academic activities that were consistent with its aims. All else was illegitimate. For Jaspers, as for Arendt, academic freedom is more than merely academic.

In the UK, we have two constitutional post-war definitions of academic freedom. For the 1963 Robbins report, it is the freedom to publish, to teach according to a teacher's own concept of fact and truth, and 'to pursue what personal studies and researches are congenial'. For Robbins, academic tenure guarantees such freedoms. When the 1988 Education Reform Act abolished tenure, it redefined academic freedom. Section 202 of the Act gave academics 'freedom within the law to question and test received wisdom, and to put forward new ideas and controversial or unpopular opinions, without placing themselves in jeopardy of losing their jobs or privileges that they may have at their institutions'.

No one seriously is suggesting the abandonment of such principles. However, thanks to the economic logic of cuts to public expenditure, we have drifted insidiously and gradually towards that dangerous state of affairs where the spectres of 'official knowledge' and 'official teaching' are increasingly visible and material. If Jaspers and Arendt are right, then our predicament may be all the worse for the fact that we fail to see our democratic liberty being threatened by a quiet ruination and decay of academic freedom.

Arendt, writing back to Jaspers after reading his book, considered what should be the proper relation between state and university: 'Because

Anti-cuts demonstration, Trafalgar Square, London, 9 November 2011
Credit: Mikael Buck/Rex Features

somebody has to pay for the whole show, the state clearly remains the best donor of money.' She continued: 'It would be good … if the professors would not, despite this, see themselves as civil servants.' Some arrangement was needed – and eventually found in the German constitution – to protect academic freedom; but, in the UK in recent times, the arrangements are different.

The first major cuts to UK university funding took place in the 1980s, as part of a project of privatisation that diminished the state's commitments to the public sphere. The demand for accountability in the public sector, for 'value for money', was crucial to the ideological acceptance of this process. Universities adopted a business-like efficiency, encapsulated in the mantra of 'doing more with less'. Success in making economies then provided the rationale for further cuts, for we were now 'doing more' than was previously thought necessary, and so could accommodate additional cutting of resources; and if we failed, we deserved to be cut entirely, for we had failed in doing what was necessary. This argument led to a rationale for what happened finally in 2010, when the UK government formally withdrew all funding for the teaching of arts, humanities and social sciences, and cut the general budget by 80 per cent following the Browne Review.

The effects of the cuts have been gradual and insidious, but substantive: we now no longer research as we wish, teach as we wish, or pursue those congenial studies that Robbins wanted to protect. Arendt's fear – that academics would become servants of their governments – was well founded. In 1992, the UK University Grants Committee (UGC) was replaced by the Higher Education Funding Councils (HEFCE) and the change of title brought into law a change of practice. Where the UGC had acted as a buffer between academy and government, to stop us becoming civil servants, HEFCE's management statement virtually required that we make our academic freedoms subservient to the state. Paragraph 3.4.2 of that statement requires that 'The Chairman [of HEFCE] is responsible to the Secretary of State. The Chairman shall aim to ensure that the HEFCE's policies and actions support the wider strategic policies of the Secretary of State.'

HEFCE became an arm of government; and, without debate, the dominos fell. Vice-chancellors became agents of HEFCE, and academics – no longer 'authorities' – became human resources in the advancement of government strategy. The university – without legislation – was now tacitly politicised, and our research and teaching legally constrained and restricted.

It is important to state that things are not always as crude as this on the ground. Academics continue to maintain their integrity and independence in their research and teaching, but this is despite the prevailing norms, and their chances of official recognition are therefore much diminished.

Yet the perception of academics as accountable to the requirements of the government of the day, rather than the demands of intellectual inquiry, has become entrenched: our main priority is to serve business and to do whatever government decides is necessary for the economy. Charles Clarke, as Secretary of State for Education, argued in 2003 that 'We have to make better progress in harnessing knowledge to wealth creation.' Consequently, the 2003 Lambert Review identified 'a need for the government to support university departments which are doing work that industry values'; and it went on to claim that 'Public funding for basic research … is intended to benefit the economy.' Later, the 2011 Wilson Review stated that 'Universities form the supply chain for business.' These views are now so commonplace that they provoke no debate.

In this now quasi-official view of the university, research and teaching that do not serve business or wealth creation are seen as luxuries; and it is equally assumed that luxuries should not be funded from the public purse. The academic who works in medieval theology or French experimental fiction is in an invidious position: the classroom work must highlight not academic issues but rather skills that are transferable to business or wealth creation. The 'luxury' of serious critical thinking on matters of theological politics or of relations between art and society – a luxury that might provoke new thought and new freedoms beyond the academy – is now less legitimate. Academic and other freedoms are being diminished, and education itself drastically impoverished.

As a result, dissident thought is sacrificed to a tacit demand for conformity. We are expected essentially to validate whatever it is that public opinion decides is the genuine or proper existing states of affairs, and thus to confirm our cultural identity. Yet as Christopher Hitchens once put it, the greatest threat to freedom of expression today is not government but a malleable public opinion. If the public is genuinely to extend our freedoms and possibilities, then such opinion needs to be subjected to critique – sometimes by the exercise of academic freedom. The loss of our freedom to critique such constructions means that our identities – and thus our possibilities in life – are essentially in the hands of others.

The point of research is not to rehearse what we know, but to explore and extend the boundaries of our ignorance and, by thus disturbing our idea of ourselves, to prise open those human possibilities that were previously undreamt of. Such ideals sit uneasily alongside the now normative corporatist ideas of accountable efficiency.

Virtually all research funding in the UK is now competitive: we bid to research councils for it, or we win it through competing in the Research Excellence Framework (REF, formerly Research Assessment Exercise). This exercise aims to concentrate research in ever decreasing numbers of institutions (thus rationalising cuts everywhere else). A good REF performance 'earns' us our future research funds; and, cast in positive terms like this, the process obscures the fact that competition is reducing the state's commitment to the total research capacity of the nation and its academies. Governments will not inflict the cuts; instead, peer review ensures that we do the government's work and cut ourselves in a form of self-harm. We are like Kafka's Joseph K, watching his executioners with their knife and realising that he is expected to wrench it from them and 'plunge it into his own breast'.

Credit: Andrew Thomson/Sector Four

Much research is published in scholarly journals. These now also have rankings, with some having higher 'impact factors' than others. Academics are effectively required to seek publication in those highly ranked places, as the journals themselves become proxies for measuring the value of research. A piece in *Physics Letters* is ranked excellent by the REF, axiomatically; recognition of excellence is harder to secure in the new upstart journals. However, all journals have their own scholarly priorities and preferences, sometimes even ideological preferences in the humanities and social sciences. To be regarded as excellent, my research must be recognised by my peers; but, if good research is by definition marked by dissidence, then such evaluations can pose awkward difficulties. The likelihood will be for research to be considered excellent precisely to the extent that it confirms the basic principles of my peers and conforms to their priorities. So, farewell freedom, as I skew my work to get it into *Physics Letters*; and thus the REF restricts the thinking behind our increasingly sclerotic research base. Crucially, universities increasingly require that academics make sure that their research conforms to that narrowed base, in order to secure more funding – more funding that will, in turn, eviscerate the now anorexic research base further, and decrease the freedom to research as we would wish. If you want the funding that comes with prestige, make sure your work fits in. Academic freedom becomes subservient to academic orthodoxy.

The process can be politicised too, as we saw in June 2010, when the coalition government's Big Society agenda became explicitly a funding priority for the research councils. At the centre of this was a political hijacking of an interdisciplinary project called 'Connected Communities', led by the Arts and Humanities Research Council (AHRC). When the AHRC held its first summit on the programme, Shearer West, the AHRC's director of research, gave a presentation which set the scene for the research programme and its funding explicitly in terms of the Big Society framework. The only other presentation archived on the AHRC website from that summit was given by Bert Provan of the Department of Communities and Local Government. His title: 'Connected Communities; or, "Building the Big Society"'. If you want funding to carry out research, make sure you centre it on serving the political agenda.

We no longer teach as we wish but according to the logic of cuts

Similar strictures afflict teaching. We no longer teach as we wish, but according to the logic of cuts and its attendant economics. Teaching, like research, is inherently unpredictable; but such unpredictability cannot be permitted in a system grounded in efficient accountability. In teaching, especially with very high tuition fees, quality must be assured by our Quality Assurance Agency (QAA). Now that all degrees are modular, thought is compartmentalised; knowledge becomes reduced to information; and learning becomes simply the managing or manipulation of that information. The economics here understands knowledge as a commodity, and not a dynamic process that might involve the changing of minds and thus also of identities. Commodities are never critical of anything, but simply available for purchase; and that purchase is intended simply to assure the consumer of his identity, to 'enrich' an already existing and settled identity. It's just that the freedom of that identity is now reduced and narrowed to matters of consumer choice between modules.

This is all the more pressing when the UK deals with the 80 to 100 per cent cut in state funding of teaching by effecting a massive tuition-fee hike whose effect is to monetise teaching and learning. Teachers are required by QAA to predict outcomes of their teaching, so that the student knows what it is that she is 'buying'. Now, all students need to be the same as well; their futures safely predicted, managed, controlled. There is no academic freedom left in teaching – unless we ignore these strictures and carry out our work essentially in clandestine and unofficial fashion.

Accountability, though seen most vividly as part of the logic of cuts, can have further unexpected repercussions. When a former University College London (UCL) student, Umar Farouk Abdulmutallab, was found to be involved in a plot to blow up a flight from Amsterdam to Detroit, Universities UK (UUK, the vice-chancellors' association) drew up a report on freedom of speech on campus. It was interesting that they felt implicated simply because Abdulmutallab had attended UCL. No doubt, he also frequented coffee shops, but there was no similarly anxious report from Starbucks. UCL, however, chose to identify freedom of speech in academia as a subject for policing, as if the university were a site of terror by association, and therefore responsible for terrorist acts.

In the UUK report, the 1988 Reform Act statement is rehearsed: academic freedom is sacrosanct 'within the law'. It is in that phrase, 'within the law', that the report finds the absolute limit of academic freedom. On one hand, this sounds eminently reasonable: the university should not encourage criminality. However, in principle, it changes the accountability of the academic again. Where Jaspers thought that the academic's accountability was to the intellectual process itself, and where REF and QAA see accountability as being political and consumerist, UUK's report makes the academic into an official, policing 'the law of the land'. But which land? In an age of globalisation especially, intellectual work knows no such borders. Further, what if the law itself is a bad law or a law that lacks legitimacy? Is it not actually incumbent on the academic to point this out and speak out about it?

UUK appears to take the view that the results of our research and teaching must be in conformity with the law of the land; but the text of the 1988 Act might properly be read as saying that our academic freedoms are themselves protected within or by the law. That is to say: the law protects us, even if what we discover calls the law into question.

In what has by now become a classic procedure, UUK has imported the logic of accountability into academia. The result is the Quisling attitude of our vice-chancellors. On one hand, some fear speaking out lest it endangers either their own self-advancement or the competitive advancement of their institution; and on the other, there are some who do not even see the dangers inherent in their quiescent compliance. Both have fully internalised the economic logic that endangers our freedoms.

Academic freedom is at the core of the democratic intellect and a free culture. It must be fought for. ❐

©Thomas Docherty
41(3): 46/54
DOI: 10.1177/0306422012456132
www.indexoncensorship.org

Thomas Docherty is professor of English and of Comparative Literature in the University of Warwick. He is the author of many books, including most recently *For the University: Democracy and the Future of the Institution* (Bloomsbury Academic), freely available under Creative Commons. He is currently writing a book called *The World, the University, the Citizen*

Next page: Polish lecturers educate students about politics and history at a time when academic censorship was rife. From Index on Censorship, *6/1978.*

ving in Libya) Sa'id Al Sayyid Habib; Mustafa
med Husein Turki; Sayyid Al Gabrati;
qiya Ali Abdul 'Al; Galal Barakat; Gama-
din Al Sharqawi; Abdul Ghani Qamar, an
r; Medhat Bakir.

s from *Le Monde*, 30 May 1978 and *Al*
r (Lebanon), 28 May 1978

☛ Poland :
year of flying

following statement was issued by the
h Society for Academic Courses, also
n as the 'Flying University', at the con-
n of its first year of educational activity.

rst year of educational self-help under the
ces of the SAC is drawing to an end.
e Society was inaugurated on 22 January
on the initiative of several dozen scho-
writers and social activists in order to
te and organise educational self-help in
ocial sciences and humanities among
students and young intellectuals.
ing the past year, the Society has sup-
the educational self-help groups which
lready in existence before its inception
s undertaken new initiatives. From Octo-
77 to May 1978 there have been more
20 educational self-help meetings in
, Cracow, Wroclaw, Lodz, and Poznan.
s and individual lessons have been
by Stefan Amsterdamski, Stanislaw
ak, Wladyslaw Bartoszewski, Czeslaw
ski, Tomasz Burek, Bohdan Cywinski,
dlicki, Tadeusz Kowalik, Jacek Kuron,
Kurowski, Edward Lipinski, Edward
, Jan Walc, Adam Michnik, Irena
wa, Adam Stanowski, Jan Strzelecki,
Szapowski, Andrzej Werner, Wiktor
lski, Karol Zarnowski, and others. The
of the lectures and seminars were post-
h history, the history of social thought,
of contemporary social structures,
questions, problems of education,
of science, philosophy, literature, and
mporary arts. The historical lectures
the greatest success; they attracted
s of a hundred and more. The more
d questions drew groups which were
t on that account more constant and
ed. All the courses started last

A typical ' flying ' course

Lecturer: Jerzy Jedlicki
Subject: Social-Political Ideologies (From
the French Revolution to the Second
World War)

1 Social functions of ideology. Ideology
   as ' false consciousness ' and as the
   aim of common aspirations.
2 Universal themes of ideology of the
   last two centuries. ' Monist ' and
   ' eclectic ' ideologies.
3 Liberalism, or the idea of freedom and
   the community of citizens.
4 Socialism, or the idea of equalising
   conditions.
5 Conservatism, or the idea of the organic community.
6 Nationalism in powerful and subjugated
   nations.
7 Communism, or the idea of revolution
   as the midwife of freedom.
8 Social democracy, or the idea of the
   welfare state.
9 Fascism, or the uniting of the masses
   with the state and government.
10 The crisis of liberal democracy and
    reformism.
11 Dialectic of extremism and compro-
    mise as the rule of ideological
    struggle.

In 1978-9 this course will be continued
as *Modern Ideology*, the subject of which
will be social ideas and movements after
the Second World War in capitalist,
socialist, and developing countries.

---

autumn commanded the interest of the students to the end. Coordination of the work
was undertaken by the Programme Committee
which was set up by the signatories of the
declaration of the Society in two successive
meetings. The Programme Committee assumed
the responsibility of selecting lecturers and
undertook to prepare the Society's programme
of educational self-help for the next year.
   A remarkable feature of the discussions during lectures and seminars was the genuine
curiosity of the young people and the maturity
of their approach to the questions being debated.
It is also important to stress their composure
and self-restraint when the conditions of edu-

CROSSING THE LINE

Turkish scholars who dare to challenge taboos may end up on trial. **Maureen Freely** assesses the climate

Derya Bayır won acclaim for her dissertation last year when it was judged one of the best on a Turkish subject by a student in Europe. Her research at Queen Mary, University of London to be published by Ashgate in 2013, links the exclusion and persecution of minorities with the state's monolithic definition of Turkishness, showing how deeply the concept is embedded in jurisprudence and the law. Despite the accolade, Derya doubts that any law faculty in Turkey will be prepared to give her a job: back home, her area of expertise is still taboo. Any academic who dedicates their career to exploring subjects that question state ideology – from the notion of Turkishness, to the legacy of Atatürk and the status of Kurdish and Armenian minorities – may fall foul of the authorities. The problem is rooted, Derya believes, in the very structure of higher education in Turkey, and most particularly the Higher Education Council (YÖK). Founded in the immediate aftermath of the 12 September 1980 coup, the most brutal in living memory, it reorganised education along strict military lines, requiring professors to instil in their students the 'national, moral, humanitarian, spiritual and cultural values of the Turkish nation', encouraging them to be 'proud and happy to be Turks', putting 'the needs of society above personal ambitions', revering Family, Country and Nation and eager to put their patriotic duties and responsibilities into practice.

All council members are appointed by the president. Those serving on its committee are appointed by the president, the committee of ministers, the council of state or the military General Staff. These are the people who set the limits of each discipline, the so-called red lines. The aim, in the words of Derya Bayır, is to prevent scholars from moving 'out of the box set by the state and the law'.

When it first came into being, YÖK cast a very long shadow. There were mass dismissals, with many other academics resigning in protest. Many thousands of lecturers and students were already in prison, and many more in exile; more now followed. But by the 1990s, when Turkey had opened its economy, also relaxing its iron control of communications, many felt sufficiently encouraged to make the return journey. The university sector was expanding rapidly, and as Turkey moved ever closer to European accession, it was again possible on the few liberal islands within the academic establishment to engage in critical scholarship on Turkish history, politics, society and literature, at least to some degree. Most academics in those fields had strong links with colleagues working in their areas in universities in North America and Europe.

Over the past 15 years, and thanks in large part to these international collaborations, there has been a great deal of important work published on

A student is detained after shouting during a debate on the government's
'Kurdish initiative', Ankara, 13 November 2009
Credit: AP Photo

the taboo areas, transforming whole disciplines within and outside Turkey, and even, in some cases, public debate. But it remains a risky enterprise. Those lower down the ladder need to be careful in their choice of words, and even in their choice of language. 'Writing in English is a safeguard,' says Kerem Öktem, research fellow at St Antony's College, Oxford. 'I have a lot of friends who've stopped writing in Turkish altogether.'

Working abroad is another safeguard, but even this does not offer full protection. In earlier years, when Öktem was a post-doctoral fellow at St Antony's, he was informed by a reliable source that the Turkish Embassy had opened a file on him which they sent to the Foreign Ministry in Ankara, accusing him of engaging in pro-Armenian (and hence anti-state) research. At the same time, a prominent Turkish university sent letters to the University of Oxford casting aspersions on his character. This did not stop him writing on forbidden or discouraged topics, or from joining the networks then reopening the debate on the Armenian genocide, but he limited what he said in print: 'Now I do more.'

The most important chair in contemporary Turkish studies in this country is at the LSE. The position is currently occupied by Şevket Pamuk, the distinguished economic historian, better known outside his field as the brother of Nobel laureate Orhan Pamuk. Like many university positions in Turkish Studies in the US, it is funded by a consortium of Turkish banks and foundations. All possess strong links to the political establishment, and that creates potential difficulties for any candidate known to have crossed the state's so-called red lines.

What some now refer to as the 'Turkish spring' was well underway when the AKP (Justice and Development Party) came to power in 2002. The party's pro-market, pro-Europe brand of Islamism seemed mild after the fiery fundamentalist rhetoric of the Islamist parties that the military had banned in previous decades. Many red-line scholars were glad to see it challenge the military and the state bureaucracies (YÖK amongst them) that continued to enforce the Kemalist brand of nationalist secularist authoritarianism. Many more were now daring to write about the Kurdish problem, the Armenian genocide and Kemalism. And yet, as Erol Köroğlu, professor of Turkish Language and Literature at Boğaziçi University, points out, there was always 'a danger of being prosecuted, going to trial because of books or articles published. The Anti-Terror Law, the infamous Article 301 and similar laws give opportunities to prosecutors who want to open lawsuits on academic or non-academic publications'.

The new religious agenda is broad and growing broader

In the early days of AKP ascendance, there was still a hope that this new anti-establishment party aimed to dismantle not just the coup-sponsored 1982 constitution but also the state bureaucracies that put it into force. What the AKP did, however, was to remove the Kemalists from these institutions and replace them with their own people. Instead of reforming these bodies, they have used them to impose their own brand of nationalist Islamist authoritarianism.

With the consolidation of power has come a sharpening of anti-secular rhetoric, never more so than when the subject is education and the proper place of religion in the curriculum. In February, Erdoğan proclaimed that it was his ambition to create a new generation of religious youth: a bald challenge to the secularists whom the prime minister has likened to 'thinning addicts'. The new religious agenda is broad and growing broader: there is the government's growing hostility to women's rights, and its recent and very sudden decision to ban abortion – never a matter for controversy until now. There is also a budding romance with creationism, which began with the government stopping TÜBITAK (the Turkish Science and Technology Research Council) from publishing a 2009 issue celebrating Darwin's 200th birthday, and at the same time sacking its editor.

The AKP has, most concede, done more than its predecessors to solve what is commonly known as the Kurdish problem, and what historian Baki Tezcan with some irony calls the Turkish problem 'because it's the Turks who have trouble recognising Kurds as real human beings'. In Mardin University, located in the country's largely south-east, there is even a Kurdish studies programme. It stays within the lines set by the state, of course. This is not enough progress for those allied with the Kurdish democratic movement, for long the most organised force of opposition in the country. Its calls for full citizenship rights for Turkish Kurds are finding ever broader support on university campuses, and a common cause with Turkish students on the left. This has led in turn to a crackdown on dissent in the university sector – not just the sacking of scholars who research on Kurdish issues, but also the arrest of thousands of students under counter-terrorism legislation, which allows for lengthy pre-trial detention. It is difficult to assess the number of students currently behind bars, but conservative estimates put it at 700.

Turkish students belonging to socialist organisations are often charged with membership of Revolutionary Headquarters, an organisation that many believe no longer exists, while Kurdish students are generally charged with membership of the KCK (Union of Communities in Kurdistan), which the government claims is the urban branch of the armed Kurdish separatist PKK (Kurdistan Workers' Party). The common understanding of this ploy is illustrated in a recent cartoon in a popular satirical magazine, featuring a KCK leader who is full of regret at not knowing what a large membership the group had, and who promises to keep better records in future.

Students have been targeted in a number of cases this year. Cihan Kırmızıgül, a Galatasaray university engineering student, was sentenced in May to 11 years for wearing a traditional Kurdish 'poshu' scarf; Şeyma

Students clash with riot police during a protest over government interference in university appointments and excessive force employed by police, Middle East Technical University, Ankara, 5 January 2011

Credit: AP Photo

Özcan, a Boğaziçi University history student, was detained last year because she applied for the same work experience position as another student charged with membership of Revolutionary Headquarters; countless others have been arrested because they attended demonstrations calling for Kurdish language rights, free university tuition and the reform of YÖK itself. In June, 90 medical students in five cities were taken into custody, under suspicion of being the medical wing of the KCK. It was alleged that they had, amongst other charges, sought to alienate the public from the government health services - this because they had been offering free blood pressure and diabetes tests in poor neighbourhoods. A student who collected 500TL (less than 200 pounds sterling) for a picnic was deemed to be the medical wing's finance officer.

There is also Büşra Ersanlı, the distinguished Marmara University professor, who was detained at the end of October 2011 on charges that were not disclosed even to her own lawyers. She became a target, most believe, because she was a member of the BDP (Peace and Democracy Party, a legal democratic Kurdish party, with seats in the national assembly) and gave lectures to its supporters. Her arrest sparked outrage throughout the academic community. Erol Köroğlu describes her as 'a perfect public intellectual, educator and academic' and a 'very successful example of intellectual responsibility'. She is being prosecuted, he says, 'because she is a conscientious and responsible intellectual. She is simply a nice person and a good Samaritan. She has worked for every democratic movement and for the development of a more democratic Turkey'. Like all 'decent academics' in Turkey, she is 'a good researcher, good social worker and a good teacher'. If she lived abroad, he says, 'she would be a very famous and effective political science person'. If nothing else, a post abroad would have allowed her to give more time to her research, and less time to defending the right to research. 'This is our fate in Turkey. You have to be a social worker, an academic, a teacher with a heavy teaching load, and a politician at the same time.'

Older academics speak of a climate of fear

After waiting nine months for her first hearing, Ersanlı was released, pending trial. The case is expected to continue for many years - which is the rule in trials like this and a means of disabling a dissident's life and career. Ersanlı had to wait until 2 July 2012 for her first hearing. The feminist sociologist Pinar Selek is still being prosecuted in connection with an explosion (allegedly a PKK bomb, but more probably a faulty gas cannister) in the Spice Bazaar in Istanbul. Despite having been acquitted in 2002, 2006 and 2010, the case continues. So too does the hate campaign: she is routinely smeared in the media, with her name turning up in accounts of KCK trials. It is widely believed that she was targeted for work she had done on Istanbul's Kurds.

These cases, and the labelling of all other forms of dissent as terrorist, have prompted older academics to speak of a climate of fear that reminds them of the early 1980s, when the military used YÖK to bend universities to its will. Others believe that what we are seeing now is the beginning of something much worse, with colleges proliferating that are no more than 'diploma factories' and red lines that promote a growing hostility to science – further complicating the assault on academic freedom. An alarming number of univerities are disciplining (and expelling) students who have been charged (but not yet found guilty) with membership of the KCK or Revolutionary Hearth.

Even Sabanci, the private university known to be the most liberal in the country, with a famously eloquent defence of free expression on its website, did not permit its students to put up posters advertising this year's May Day demonstrations, on account of their carrying, albeit in the tiniest print, the logo of the (legal) BDP. University rectors appear to be afraid or unwilling to stand up to YÖK: conferences and seminars that their new masters may view as seditious are cancelled and even repudiated.

Despite the intimidation, the anger on campuses is visible and growing. University lecturers have set up an organisation called 'Don't Touch My Student' while another group, the Initiative for Solidarity with Arrested Students, has undertaken to count and map the students now in detention. There is also GIT (the Transnational Work Group on Academic Liberty and Freedom of Research in Turkey), a loose-knit web of scholars inside and outside Turkey that began in France late last year and now has chapters in the US and England. (I am a signatory). Back home, it has been campaigning fiercely for Büşra Ersanlı while also working hard to draw attention to the hundreds of prisoners whose names we do not yet know. Its Turkish chapter has run an open-air lecture series outside prisons, and, in alliance with the other above-mentioned networks, as well as its own European and American chapters, it is trying to alert the outside world to the crisis.

It is, in a sense, picking up where an earlier electronic network, left off: WATS, the Workshop for Turkish/Armenian Scholarship, which operated out of the University of Michigan, connecting more than 700 scholars, journalists, writers, and activists, during the first decade of this century. Faciliated by the Turkish-born scholar Müge Göçek, its aim was to create a space for the proper scholarly discussion of the Armenian genocide, linking all those inside Turkey with an interest in the issue with scholarly debates abroad. And so it did. But in the long run, and as much thanks to its stormier seasons as its calm ones, it did a great deal more. It pulled red-line scholars out of isolation, drawing them into an international community of like-minded researchers and thinkers. Whenever they were harrassed, intimidated, and prosecuted, this community responded quickly to campaign on their behalf. Whether researching the Armenian genocide or Ottoman and republican history, scholars would sooner or later collide with the red lines protecting state ideology.

As with so many electronic networks, a moment arrived when the centre could not hold. But in all the countries where its participants lived and worked, it had by then fostered social networks of scholars that have lasted. These have gone on to foster a new generation of scholars. In the past, says Müge Göçek, most Turks studying abroad went into the sciences, engineering or medicine. But now she is seeing an increasing number of students going abroad to do critical work on the Armenian and Kurdish issues, gender issues and the law. Whatever obstacles they might encounter along the way, these younger scholars will inevitably change the face of work on Turkey: 'The dominant discourse outside Turkey will no longer reproduce the official line.'

What happens inside Turkey also seems predictable, so long as YÖK persists in its current form. When red-line scholars in Turkish universities challenge the state – newly Islamicised, but as nationalist and authoritarian as ever – they will need the support of like-minded colleagues abroad. But there are problems here, too, as Baki Tezcan, one of the founders of the American chapter of GIT, pointed out to me. Back in February, when Prime Minister Erdoğan proclaimed his intention to create a new generation of religious youth, a Facebook group helped circulate a petition of protest that garnered 3,014 signatures. When the group then proposed a YouTube version, in which signatories would take turns reading lines from their letter of protest, each and every signatory they approached inside Turkey came back with the same response: they were honoured to have been asked, and of course they would have liked to participate, but if they took part in a protest in such a public arena, they would be putting their research projects, their careers, and even their futures, at risk.

Tezcan tells me this story to illustrate not just the constraints on his colleagues in Turkey, but also the importance of working together to find a way through. When I visited YouTube, I was impressed by the sophistication of their solution. Nine unnamed scholars based overseas take turns to recite the letter of protest: we then see the names of the 3,014 signatories, and the number of hits – 118,846. The figure of 100,000 was reached in the first week, I'm told. It is yet another sign that, whatever the structures of the state, and however much it wishes to stamp out dissent, expectations amongst students and young scholars are rising. 'Turkey is so proud to be part of the G20,' says Baki Tezcan. 'Why not also be proud to be one of the world's top democracies? We need to ask for more. We deserve more.'

It remains to be seen if scholars based in Turkey and abroad can continue to organise effectively – veterans of WATS will remember the many ways in which electronic networks can be manipulated and kept under surveillance by fake friends with agendas. But the fight for academic freedom in Turkey has well and truly broken through the lines set by the state. It is electronic and international and will be hard, perhaps impossible, to quell. ❒

©Maureen Freely
41(3): 56/65
DOI: 10.1177/0306422012456477
www.indexoncensorship.org

Maureen Freely is a novelist, translator and lecturer at the University of Warwick. Her novels include *Enlightenment* (Marion Boyars)

For further reading:

Baki Tezcan (2010) *The Second Ottoman Empire: Political and Social Transformation in the Early Modern World* (Cambridge University Press)

Kerem Öktem (2011) *Turkey since 1989: Angry Nation* (Zed Books)

Fatma Müge Göçek (2011) *The Transformation of Turkey: Redefining State and Society from the Ottoman Empire to the Modern Era* (IB Tauris)

Erol Köroğlu (2007) *Ottoman Propaganda and Turkish Identity: Literature in Turkey during World War I* (IB Tauris)

Derya Bayır (forthcoming, 2013) *Minorities and Nationalism in Turkish Law* (Ashgate)

CRY FOR PEACE

Amy Spangler introduces work by one of Turkey's most celebrated Kurdish writers **Mehmed Uzun**, who fought for the right to express himself

Academic freedom is hardly possible without freedom of expression, and there can be no freedom of expression when restrictions are placed upon the use of a language, let alone when an entire language is banned. In Turkey, Kurdish was first prohibited in 1924, and continued to be banned for much of the 20th century. Though restrictions on the language have been relaxed in recent years, its usage still remains a point of contention. Demands for education in the mother tongue have so far met with small concessions. The current government recently stated its intention to make education in the mother tongue available as an elective course at the 5th grade. However, it remains to be seen whether or not this will come to fruition, and even if it does come to pass, many, myself included, maintain that it is not enough. After all, as a result of decades of a ban that ranges from enforcement to strict discouragement, generations of Kurds, not to mention other minorities, have been alienated from their mother tongue.

Even for novelist and essayist Mehmed Uzun (1953-2007), the most prominent and prolific founder of modern Kurdish literature, alienation from the mother tongue was a stark reality. Uzun describes his early childhood as a kind of paradise in which he was surrounded by storytellers, bearers of a rich oral tradition that would later inform Uzun's own literary style, as you will see in the excerpt on the following pages. His first day at school was the beginning of his descent from that paradise. It was 'the first step I took away from my heaven towards hell', he wrote in his memoir *Ruhun Gökkuşağı*. On his first day at school, he would be served a slap for not singing along with the national anthem. But then how could he? He didn't even know Turkish, let alone the anthem. Uzun writes: As the slap exploded on my face, lightning struck in my soul; that's right, not on my face, in my soul'. The sting of that slap would stay with him, and it would later become one of the driving forces compelling him to become a Kurdish novelist, writing in Kurdish, at a time when the Kurdish novel was, for the most part, unheard of.

It was not until Uzun reached the age of 19, while in prison for writing leftist graffiti, that he first saw his mother tongue in written form, and that he 'first fell in love with that impossible language, the source of my pain and my pleasure'. It should be noted that technically Uzun's mother tongue, ie his mother's first language, was not the dominant dialect of Kurdish in which he would later write, Kurmanji, but the dialect Kirmanjki or Zazaki (which is considered a separate language by some and is now endangered).

After being released, he became the managing editor of a Kurdish-Turkish newspaper, which soon landed him in prison once again on charges of separatism. After escaping to Sweden in 1977, where he would live in exile until 2005, Uzun began writing his first novel in Kurdish. Six more would follow. Uzun and his publishers would be put on trial again and again for inciting separatism. As anyone who has actually read Uzun's literature can tell you, however, his work provokes many feelings, above all sadness, longing, and melancholy, and they most certainly cause one to question the historical narrative that dominates history books in Turkey, but they are not a cry for war – to the contrary, they are a cry for peace.

The struggle that Mehmed Uzun so valiantly undertook continues today. It is the struggle for freedom of expression. It is the struggle for the right to live and love and write in the mother tongue, to foster that language and see it thrive in prose and poetry. We owe it to Mehmed Uzun to carry forth that struggle.

The following excerpt is from the novel *Ronî Mîna Evîne, Tarî Mîna Mirinê* (Luminous Like Love, Dark Like Death). Set in an unnamed yet familiar geography, this suspenseful yet lyrical novel tells the story of Baz and Kevok, two characters who share a homeland, yet whose lives take very different paths. At the beginning of the novel we find Baz and Kevok together in a van,

Mehmed Uzun
Credit: Ulla Montan

being taken to their execution. In subsequent chapters, we learn each character's individual story, and how it is they have come to meet with such a fate.

In this extract, we read of an attack on Baz's village, when Baz is still very young. It is only much later that Baz, a notoriously ruthless professional soldier engaged in warfare against guerilla fighters, such as Kevok, in the mountainous region, finds out about his roots, and that he is not at all who he thinks he is. In fact, he is one of *them*.

They raise their rifles, slide bullets into barrels, and scan the surroundings. Two of them walk over to a young man lying on the ground. But before they are able to reach him, the sound of another explosion rises and echoes in the mountains. Then, quickly, one after another, in unison, flawless. Then, the sound of mitrailleuse bullets exploding on all sides. The brave young men fall, one by one – before they can even reach for their guns, before they can shoot a single bullet. In place of the water, which once glittered and gleamed and gushed, now flows blood. Blood flows from the brave young men scattered on the ground. Some of the others try to leave the cave too, but it's too late. Inside, they lie piled on top of one another, like chickens in a coop, cramped and crowded.

And they, that is, the strangers, they appear, one by one, line by line, from behind the trees, the stones, the slopes, the heights, the ruins, the rocks, all the hiding places. With their guns and bandoleers full of bullets, dressed in their light green clothes, the soldiers gradually narrow in on the cave. They are many, countless. They are everywhere, the foreigners. A few commanders who stand on either side of the cave, at some distance, give orders to the countless soldiers. At the mouth of the cave a few bullets explode, that's all, and then, now, no more sound. The foreigners silence them, don't let them react. From all sides the foreigners rain bullets into the mouth of the cave. Ceaselessly, incessantly. First with rifles, then with mitrailleuse, and then from afar, with small cannons. Again and again.

Until noon, until the sun comes and stands above the cave and its light shines like a mirror on the stomach of the stream, the explosions continue. There is no sound from inside, from inside the cave. It is as if there is no life, not a sound, not a breath, not a sign. Only a few wooden toys and a few carpets lying in front of the cave, the smoke still rising from them, indicate the existence of those inside.

In the afternoon the soldiers gradually gather at the mouth of the cave, make a pile of twigs and dry grass, and set it on fire. The mouth of the cave is covered in fire, smoke, and fumes.

Twigs, sticks, brush, dry grass, and fire. Twigs, sticks, brush, dry grass, and fire. And smoke and fumes. And the occasional explosion of mitrailleuse and cannons.

Roaring fire emerging from the barrels of the mitrailleuse and the cannons … Two cannons, one on either side of the mouth of the cave, rain down fire and death …

Towards evening, when the now reddish sun reaches the other side of the valley, the soldiers stop. The soldiers are tired. Suddenly, it is calm once again. But the pristine, serene surroundings have been turned into a war zone. This hidden paradise has been turned into hell. The trees are on fire, smoke rises from all around the cave. The bodies of sheep and goats, cattle and horses, all around, everywhere, thrashing. It's hot, very hot. The explosion of the rifles, mitrailleuse, and cannons has turned the world into a fiery lump of coal. Now there is no longer the sound of birds and wild animals, or the smell of roses and wild flowers. Only the smell of gunpowder, blood, ash, smoke and fumes. Only the smell of death.

The commanders and the soldiers, their fingers on the triggers of their guns and rifles, slowly approach the mouth of the cave. But no one enters; they wait and listen for sounds coming from the cave. But there's no sound; smoke emerges from the cave, but no sound. It's all over now … now, none of it is any use, hiding, waiting, hoping, longing, sadness, doubt, fear, nor any of the other states of desperate people, none of it is any use. Over, it's all over.

But the next moment something happens, the stuff of legends; through the smoke of the mouth of the cave, a dark figure emerges. A small puppy walks out of the smoke, letting out a barely audible yelp. Behind the puppy follows another dark figure; a small child, taking wobbly steps.

The child, two, two and a half years old, emerges from the cave, silent, with fear on its face and in its eyes. The child is a boy. He wears an animal skin and his hair is cut short. He reeks of sweat, smoke, and urine. His face is small, his eyes are small like lentil beans. When his eyes land on the commander and the soldiers, he raises his hand and tries to say something, but his voice won't come out. One of the commanders loads a bullet into his rifle and holds the rifle to the boy's head. 'No person, no sign, no voice, no trace, no path leading back, nothing should remain of them,' he says. That's what the commander thinks. The boy has no knowledge of who the commander is, or of his thoughts; he places his hand on the back of the mottled pup and pets it. But another commander, the one with an upturned, pointy moustache, doesn't allow the boy to be killed.

The commander with the pointy moustache lifts the boy, embraces him, and with his right hand, smiling, strokes the boy's small head. The child looks at the commander with expressionless eyes.

That's right, that child is Baz.

That's right, thus begins the story of Baz. ❏

©Mehmed Uzun

41(3): 67/72

DOI: 10.1177/0306422012457747

www.indexoncensorship.org

Translated from the Kurdish by Amy Spangler, with thanks to Muhtesim Güvenç for his invaluable assistance during the translation process. *Ronî Mîna Evîne, Tarî Mîna Mirinê* (Luminous Like Love, Dark Like Death) is published by İthaki Yayınları

12) WOMEX

THE WORLD MUSIC EXPO

World & Jazz Networking

Trade Fair

Showcase Festival

Conference

Networking

Film Market

Awards

virtualWOMEX

Thessaloniki, Greece
17–21 Oct 2012
www.womex.com

LOSING THE DEBATE

Protest and open discussion are under attack in Israeli universities. **Yousef T Jabareen** looks at recent threats to academic freedom

Over the past few years, the attack on Israeli academic freedom has taken two main forms: threats to students' freedom to organise politically-oriented activities on university premises and attacks on faculty who voice their criticism of government policies. The Democracy Project of the Association for Civil Rights in Israel (ACRI), one of the leading civil and human rights groups in the country, published a report covering 2010-11, warning of severe threats to academic freedom; arguably the situation is getting worse.

In recent months, the debate has centred on acknowledging – be it through political action or classroom discussion – the Nakba. The word means 'catastrophe' in Arabic, and it refers to the events leading up to and immediately following Israel's formation as a state in 1948 and the impact on the Palestinian community residing there at the time of its formation. The events range from exile from land and homes to violence and even massacre. The mere use of the word 'Palestinian' is met with criticism by many defenders of Israeli government policies, as the assertion that these events were immoral, illegal or even real. Rather than allow a healthy debate on the wealth of facts and information available on the subject, the Israeli government and

Israeli academic institutions have chosen to shut down the debate entirely, going so far as to levy sanctions on those who engage in it.

The 'Nakba law', which was passed in March 2011, is the culmination of efforts by various lobbies and members of the Knesset, Israel's parliament, to erase the subject from public discussion. It amends the national budget law to allow the minister of finance to reduce government funding to any institution (including schools and universities, community centres and local governments) that commemorates either independence day or the anniversary of the establishment of the state of Israel as a day of mourning ('Nakba day'), rejects the existence of Israel as a Jewish and democratic state, incites racism, violence or terrorism, supports armed struggle or terror activities or terrorist organisations against the state, or that vandalises or dishonours the state flag or its symbols. The minister may reduce funding by several times the cost of the activity that is deemed to be in violation of the law.

The law that was eventually passed represents a far more moderate version of the original one proposed in July 2009, which, among other things, would have made participation in events commemorating the Nakba punishable by three years' imprisonment. Still, the original law was clearer and more comprehensible. One of the most damaging aspects of the current law is its utter vagueness and broadness, so that it is difficult to anticipate what types of activities the minister of the treasury could interpret as a rejection of the 'Jewish and democratic' character of the state, or as dishonouring state symbols. One can imagine that the minister, should he choose to impose sanctions, could find a violation of the law in virtually any critique of the state, whether it be political or artistic expression. The act would not need to constitute vandalism, encourage violence or support terror in order to be compromised.

This vagueness causes a severe chilling effect among Israeli educators, leaders and students and creates uncertainty around what constitutes prohibited speech, leading to self-censorship. It is precisely the sort of law that the United States Supreme Court, in the 1950s, identified as curbing free speech – even speech that is permissible – for fear of breaking the law.

In May 2011, the alumni association of an Arab high school in Haifa, the parents of students at an Arab-Jewish school in the Galilee and a university professor, all of whom commemorate the Nakba, organise events or publish literature critiquing the 'Jewish and democratic' nature of the state, petitioned the Israeli High Court of Justice with the assistance of human rights NGOs Adalah and ACRI. They claimed that they were all at risk of losing funding and that the minister of finance could deem their

An Israeli Arab student commemorates Nakba day at Tel Aviv University, 14 May 2012
Credit: Jack Guez/AFP/Getty Images

activities to be in violation of the law. They also claimed the Nakba law was unconstitutional and its implementation would violate their freedom of expression, right to equality and free choice in education, right to freedom of occupation and the right to group dignity. Furthermore, they argued that as long as the grounds for implementation of the law remain unclear, it chills all speech critical of the state and its policies, which renders it even more dangerous to free speech in a democratic society. The court, however, dismissed the petition in January, leaving the law intact and citing the fact that the petitioners had not brought a specific case of implementation before it and thus it could not rule on its constitutionality.

Although the law has yet to be implemented by the minister of the treasury, the chilling effect is evident. Academic institutions have used it as justification for censoring faculty and students. In May 2012, during the week of the anniversary of the establishment of the state of Israel, several student groups at major Israeli universities planned events acknowledging Nakba day, some of them featuring poetry recital and prayers. Tel Aviv University granted a permit for an event to take place on university premises. However, it gave permission on the condition that event organisers pay the six security guards hired for the occasion, citing the Nakba law as grounds for placing the financial burden on the students rather than on the institution. From a civil rights perspective, forcing students to bear the costs of protest was inappropriate given that their actions were legal, even under the law. The commemoration should have been treated the same as any other event where views are freely expressed: the protection of staff and students would normally be funded by the university, or, if the event took place off campus, handled by the police. This event should not have been an exception.

Following the university's approval, a heated debate in the Knesset education committee ensued and the university was subjected to immense pressure from the minister of education, Gideon Saar, who personally called the Tel Aviv University president, requesting him to put a stop to it. In fact, the debate continued even as the event had already begun on 14 May. It stirred such emotions that the 400 students and faculty attending were met by about 200 right-wing protesters. The counter-protest included the use of a megaphone, whereas the Nakba event participants were prohibited from doing the same. Angry right-wing protesters held up signs that read 'Nakba Harta' (Nakba bullshit), called demonstrators 'traitors', shouted 'death to terrorists' and attempted to tear their signs and otherwise disrupt the event.

The censorship on Haifa University's campus was even more severe. On 16 May, it cancelled the Nakba day event organised by university students and scheduled to take place on campus, despite the fact that the necessary permits had been granted. Prior to the decision to cancel, the university administration had begun placing various restrictions on the event, which was to include a performance by artist Saleem Dou from the play Sagh Saleem, together with left-wing student activist Saar Saqali. The university banned the distribution of flyers with the word 'Nakba' and forbade Saqali from participating or even coming on to campus. According to the event organisers, the university's last-minute cancellation was influenced by pressure from both the minister of education, similar to that levied on Tel Aviv University days before, and from the National Student Union.

Student unions on university campuses have become a source of censorship themselves in recent years, as right-wing student groups have risen in popularity and strength, mirroring and encouraged by the expansion of extreme right-wing parties in the Knesset, especially since the 2009 election. One group in particular, Im Tirtzu, which has made a lot of noise both on and off campuses, is backed by substantial external funding and other resources (particularly from the Jewish Agency for Israel, according to *Calcalist* newspaper). The group was established in 2006, following Israel's second invasion of Lebanon, and purports to 'combat' the de-legitimisation of Israel and 'renew' Zionist discourse and ideology in order to 'ensure the future of the Jewish nation and the State of Israel'. Im Tirtzu has a presence on every major campus in Israel, lobbies the Knesset and publishes reports, attempting to discredit the work and funding sources of Israeli human rights NGOs and expose the 'anti-Zionist bias' among academics in Israeli institutions. The group has been successful in gaining media attention and public support, at times even through unorthodox or aggressive means, and it seems university administrations now find themselves kowtowing to its pressures and demands, particularly given the group's political leverage among Knesset members and vocalised backing by such politicians as Minister Saar.

For instance, in March, Im Tirtzu launched a campaign against Tel Aviv University philosophy professor Dr Anat Matar for her participation in a demonstration against Israel's administrative detention of Palestinian prisoners. The group initiated a student petition and organised dozens of students to file complaints against her to the university, after which the university announced that it would conduct a full investigation into her conduct. A similar campaign was launched earlier in the year against Professor Yehuda Shenhav, also of Tel Aviv University, for statements he made in his anthropology class.

In December 2009, an organisation calling itself Academia Monitor published a list of Israeli academics who supposedly wish to 'destroy the state of Israel', including academics who support the Boycott, Divestment and Sanctions (BDS) movement against Israel or who work with civil and human rights organisations such as B'tselem. In 2010, Im Tirtzu, among others, waged a campaign against politics and government professor Neve Gordon at Ben Gurion University in Beer Sheva, primarily in response to his August 2009 *Los Angeles Times* opinion piece expressing his support for BDS. The Israeli consular general accused Professor Gordon of having crossed the line of academic freedom and of joining a campaign against the state of Israel. Only when Professor Gordon received a death threat did the Ben Gurion University president come to his defence.

Although right-wing views and support of Israel's policies are mainstream in Israeli society today – both in thought and practice – groups like Im Tirtzu behave as if those voices are silenced while left-wing and critical views dominate. At best, they believe that the opposition's discourse must

Avigdor Lieberman, leader of Yisrael Beiteinu, left, and Likud parliament member and minister of education Gideon Saar at the Knesset, Jerusalem, 30 March 2009
Credit: Sebastian Scheiner/ AP Photo

be balanced, and, at worst, quashed entirely. The government seems to share this warped perception: in June, a new version of the Nakba law was proposed by a member of the extreme right-wing secular party Yisrael Beitanu. Under the proposal, the authority to implement the law would be transferred from the minister of finance to the minister of education. The bill is a clear attempt to transfer authority to a minister who will be more active in his implementation of the law, including against universities, as the minister of education also serves as the chairman of the Council for Higher Education.

This is the same education minister who just weeks earlier declared his intention to punish Israeli academics who support a boycott of Israeli academic institutions as part of the BDS movement, despite a petition signed by over 540 Israeli academics demanding that he refrain from taking actions which would curb their academic freedom. This is the same minister of education who publicly supports Im Tirtzu and who vehemently opposed Tel

Aviv University's decision to allow the ceremony commemorating Nakba day on 14 May. The bill was proposed against the recommendation of the Knesset legal advisor, who advised that it was unconstitutional and that it negated the democratic values of freedom of political speech and academic freedom. If passed, the newly revised bill would grant the minister the authority to reduce funding from academic institutions that allow any activity that negates Israel's existence as a 'Jewish and democratic state'.

In fact, the Nakba law does not stand alone. Over the past two years, right-wing parties, with the support of the government, have managed to pass a number of new laws which openly violate the rights of the Arab-Palestinian minority and infringe the freedom of speech and academic freedom rights of Arab and Jewish citizens, lay people, students and professors alike; others are still in draft form or have reached the preliminary stages of the voting process. This includes the 'boycott law', which makes it possible to launch a civil suit against anyone in Israel who calls for a boycott against the state, or even against settlements or their products – whether or not any damages can be proved. This law, too, has yet to be used but has effectively chilled speech related to boycott. Other laws set additional barriers: for example, laws pertaining to 'admissions committees' that decide whether Arab-Palestinians can purchase houses in certain towns or a law that allows citizenship to be stripped from anyone who commits 'treason' or 'aids an enemy state in a time of war', part of a series of what many Knesset members dub the 'loyalty laws'. Israel's political majority is exploiting its numeric advantage to infringe on the rights of the minority and, consequently, is creating an atmosphere of tyranny of the majority.

Today right-wing politicians are busy politicising what can be published and said in universities, yet little attention is paid to what is not expressed. It is hardly more political to discuss the events leading up to the formation of the State of Israel and its impact on the Palestinian-Arab community than it is to refrain from acknowledging such an impact entirely. In June 2011, a mandatory curriculum introducing a focus on former Israeli prime ministers Menachem Begin and David Ben-Gurion as national leaders was introduced for all schools, including Arab schools. Yet no Arab leaders are included in the mandatory curriculum, despite the fact that Arab-Palestinians comprise nearly 20 per cent of Israel's population.

What to teach and what not to teach in higher education can be a profoundly political choice across a spectrum of disciplines, from law to psychology to literature, and censoring the minority opinion, particularly in the ostensibly democratic institution of academia, can never be the answer.

When academics start being fearful of expressing their views in the dark shadow of political pressure and the threat of delegitimisation, academic freedom is at serious risk. Moreover, the absence of a full presentation of all perspectives of historic and present events not only silences segments of society, but it hinders the realisation of the full potential of the minority, thereby stunting the growth of society as a whole. ❐

©Yousef T Jabareen
41(3): 74/81
DOI: 10.1177/0306422012456142
www.indexoncensorship.org

Yousef T Jabareen is a law lecturer at the University of Haifa and Tel-Hai Academic College and the founder and general director of Dirasat, the Arab Center for Law and Policy, based in Nazareth. Thanks to Emily Schaeffer for her contribution to this article

NEW FROM SEAGULL BOOKS

manifestos for the 21st century

EDITED BY URSULA OWEN AND JUDITH VIDAL-HALL

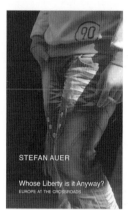

JUST PUBLISHED

Whose Liberty is it Anyway?

EUROPE AT THE CROSSROADS

STEFAN AUER

PB, 4.25" X 7", 120PP., $9.50 / £6

ISBN 978 0 8574 2 040 4

Europe's turn of fortune is humbling, humiliating and, perhaps, irreversible. What went wrong, and when? Old questions have now acquired new meaning: Is it possible to maintain conditions for selfgovernment while undermining the nation-state? What are the limits of solidarity? Can Europe be truly united through its common history, or its common currency? Is further unity in Europe even desirable?

JUST PUBLISHED

Beyond the Wall

WRITING A PATH THROUGH PALESTINE

BIDISHA

PB, 4.25" X 7", 120PP., $9.50 / £6

ISBN 978 0 8574 2 039 8

Their voices come from Bethlehem and Hebron. You can hear them from Jerusalem to Nazareth, and witness their protests in Gaza and Ramallah. From the refugee camps in the West Bank, you can hear the voices of the Palestinian people call out to demand self-determination and a better quality of life. But outside of Israel and the occupied territories, these individual voices are rarely heard—until now.

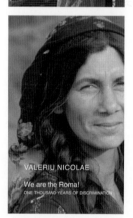

FORTHCOMING IN OCTOBER 2012

We are the Roma!

ONE THOUSAND YEARS OF DISCRIMINATION

VALERIU NICOLAE

PB, 4.25" X 7", 120PP., $9.50 / £6

ISBN 978 0 8574 2 038 1

The violent discrimination and ghettoization of Roma communities continue today inside the EU despite legislation designed to protect them against racism.no country or official body has taken up the case of the Roma and strongly argued for their protection and integration. Valeriu Nicolae, himself a Romanian Roma, gives voice to the Roma cause, offering a precise and candid look at their current situation.

TRADE ENQUIRIES TO UPM, 0117 9020275
DISTRIBUTED BY JOHN WILEY, 1243 779777
FOR THE UNIVERSITY OF CHICAGO PRESS
www.press.uchicago.edu

LONDON NEW YORK CALCUTTA

www.seagullbooks.org

A QUESTION OF SOURCES

Police are demanding a university archive hand over confidential interviews for a murder inquiry. **Michael Foley** explores an ethical conflict

At first sight, Boston College's Belfast Project is an oral history programme designed in some sort of historians' heaven: protagonists from both sides of the Northern Ireland political divide willing to talk about their involvement in politics and violence to researchers under strict confidentiality. Add to that the fact that the researchers were award-winning journalist and author Ed Moloney, who has covered the North for *The Irish Times* and the Dublin-based *Sunday Tribune*; Anthony McIntyre, PhD, a Ballymurphy republican and former IRA prisoner; and Wilson McArthur, a Shankill Road former Progressive Unionist Party activist and political science graduate of Queen's University, and you have a mix that offered scholarly rigour with journalistic engagement and a deep understanding of the issues and people being researched.

Now the project has become mired in a mix of politics, ethics and the law, with the Northern Ireland police trying to get hold of the archive and appeals are being made for the intervention of the Secretary of State, Hillary Clinton, and the US Attorney General, Eric Holder.

The project started in 2001 when some 40 or so paramilitaries and activists were interviewed over the next five years, according to *Boston College* magazine. The interviewees were people who had lived and fought through 30 years of political violence, either on the republican or loyalist side. Those interviewed were given a guarantee that material would be held securely in Boston College's Burns Library until the interviewees died or consented to their interviews being made public.

Voices From the Grave: Two Men's War in Ireland by Ed Moloney, published in 2010, was the first material to be made public, following the deaths of Brendan Hughes, former IRA commander, prisoner and hunger striker, and David Ervine, former UVF member and member of the Northern Ireland Assembly for the Progressive Unionist Party. The book relied heavily on the interviews, giving it authority and authenticity, with Moloney providing context and a narrative.

Hughes, a controversial figure, was responsible for some of the most violent events of the Troubles. He believed the Good Friday Agreement, and the compromises that entailed, meant he lost everything he had fought for and that his former comrades, especially his friend Gerry Adams, had sold out. Ervine, on the other hand, steered the UVF towards ceasefire and believed he and his community emerged out of the troubles with a stronger union with Britain.

The book offered insights into what made the two men do what they did. There was no doubt that the Brendan Hughes half of the book is the most riveting. Ervine is more restrained, telling us little if anything about what he did while in the UVF before being arrested. Hughes, on the other hand, appears to be completely honest and saw this project as his only chance to tell his story. We learn why he joined the IRA, how he was trained, what life was like for an IRA volunteer, and then commander, how decisions were taken, what life was like in Long Kesh prison, along with the blanket protest and later the hunger strikes. He also explains the morality that guided him. And we learn about Gerry Adams.

Adams has always denied he was ever a member of the IRA. Not only does Hughes say he was a member, but that he was Hughes's commanding officer. But worse than membership, which so many people assume anyway, Hughes accused Adams of ordering the killing of Jean McConville, a Belfast mother of ten, in 1972, a claim Adams has always denied. Jean McConville's body was finally discovered on a beach in Co Louth in 2003, having been unearthed by a storm.

Jean McConville is alleged to have been an informer, a charge Hughes believes, so her killing is not Hughes's main issue – killing is what happened to informers. Her body was buried and was not found at the time of her death, so she became one of the 'disappeared'. For Hughes that makes it a murder. To have left her body to be found would have been a warning to others, and that is the only reason to kill an informer, he maintained.

Meanwhile, another interviewee, Dolours Price, convicted of car bombing the Old Bailey in London in 1973, was mentioned in a Belfast paper in connection with the allegation of Gerry Adams's involvement in the McConville disappearance. A newspaper claimed its reporter knew what she had told the Boston College researchers concerning the disappearance of Jean McConville. That led to the Police Service of Northern Ireland's (PSNI) demand for material held in the archive relating to the death and disappearance of McConville.

If anyone thought such a demand would take years they were sadly mistaken because of the mutual legal assistance treaty between the UK and the US. The treaty, which was signed as part of the war on terrorism, to allow suspects to be moved from one country to another, was now invoked. Anthony McIntyre is reported to have asked at a recent oral history conference why Boston College, with its law school, did not know about the treaty and its possible impact.

The PSNI's reasons for attempting to gain access to academic material in a US university archive was not a huge mystery. On the face of it, the request was a simple one: they were trying to solve an old case and bring to justice a terrorist group guilty of murdering a mother and then burying her body, so her family could not even mourn her passing. Eamonn McCann, in the publication *Counter Punch*, suggested that old RUC officers, still smarting over the disappearance of their beloved police force, saw this as an opportunity to get Gerry Adams, who they blamed for its demise.

On the other hand, one might think a major university would defend its academic integrity and fight the case, and even point out it was not Boston College's role to investigate crimes for the PSNI. That did not happen.

To the dismay of Ed Moloney and Anthony McIntyre, Boston College decided not to contest a lower-court order to hand the tapes over. Maloney and McIntyre have decided to take their case to the US Supreme Court. They will argue that the mutual legal assistance treaty gives greater powers to foreign agencies than it does to American agencies such as the FBI. They will also state that they want their rights under the First Amendment taken into account. The famous endorsement of freedom of the press applies equally to academic freedom, according to a statement issued by Ed Moloney and Anthony McIntyre. However, they also maintain that the judgment has turned the case into a political issue that should be considered by the attorney general and the secretary of state. Moloney has stated that since the Court has ruled, either or both the secretary of state and attorney general can now act and kill the subpoenas without any further recourse to the US courts at all.

Anthony McIntyre, Drogheda, Ireland, 13 January 2012
Credit: Peter Morrison/AP Photo

Meanwhile, McIntyre has taken the case to the UK with a decision to challenge the PSNI using the Human Rights Act and the European Convention on Human Rights. The European Court on Human Rights ruled in favour of journalistic source confidentiality, in the landmark case *Goodwin v UK* in 1996.

The defence offered by Ed Moloney and Anthony McIntyre conflates journalistic ethics with academic ethics and freedoms. Moloney has no doubt about where his ethics lie. In an email interview he said: 'I always regarded this in exactly the same light as a journalistic enterprise, not least because some time in the future I might be writing about the contents, so yes, that principle underlined the project.'

Even if Boston College was not prepared to defy the law, by moving the archive out of the jurisdiction for instance, Moloney insists that the college assured him and Anthony McIntyre that it would be legally impossible to gain access to the files and that the researchers' assurances to the interviewees were perfectly legal: 'We went forward with the assurance from [Boston College] that this was not a legal possibility [to demand the files]. However, once the subpoenas were served, I expected [Boston College] to resist to the utmost. In that regard we have been terribly disappointed. They abandoned the field after the first legal reverse when they should have insisted on appealing this as far as legally possible, ie to the Supreme Court.'

For journalists, the issue is uncomplicated. Defending sources is absolute. There is not a code of ethics anywhere that does not call in the strongest terms for a journalist always to maintain the anonymity of a confidential source. For instance, the National Union of Journalists of Britain and Ireland's code of conduct states categorically: 'A journalist shall protect confidential sources of information.' Contrast that with other clauses that contain qualifying statements such as 'subject to the justification by overriding considerations of the public interest'. Similarly, the International Federation of Journalists' code, which is often used as a model for journalists' codes in emerging democracies, states: 'The journalist shall observe professional secrecy regarding the source of information obtained in confidence.'

For Moloney, this is exactly the same issue, and he has been supported by a number of American journalism organisations, including the Committee for the Protection of Journalists and the Reporters Committee for Freedom of the Press. He has also received some academic support.

While such a ringing declaration of source protection does not exist to the same unequivocal and absolutist way in academia, there are concerns about a chilling effect on research. A participant at one oral history seminar recently commented that while they talked about confidentiality and agreements with interviewees on the use of the material, there was no mention of the 'elephant in the room', the Belfast Project.

The US government's views are clear. A year ago, the Justice Department stated in a brief that researchers should not expect a court to respect confidentiality pledges made to interview subjects, and that academic freedom was not a defence. Clifford M Kuhn, a historian at Georgia State University who is a past president of the Oral History Association, filed an affidavit on behalf of Boston College in which he said that if Britain's request was granted, the field of oral history could be damaged. Quoted in the publication *Inside Higher Ed*, he said in his brief: 'Trust and rapport are at the very core of the oral history enterprise.' As part of the process of 'informed consent', interview subjects request certain levels of confidentiality, and researchers approve them. 'The reason for this protocol is to foster candor and openness in the interview itself, so as to most fruitfully and fully enhance the historical record.'

The Belfast Project does highlight a development that appears to have been taking place quietly for some time, a merging of academic and journalistic research methods and practices in certain areas. Academics are taking on subjects that might have been the preserve of journalists in the past and journalists are producing books with an increasing degree of academic respectability. Technology is speeding things up and journalists are trained to respond quickly. Journalism itself has entered the academy and is having an impact on how research is undertaken in certain areas and also how quickly it sees the light of day.

Dr Diarmaid Ferriter, one of Ireland's foremost historians, suggests some caution should be invoked: 'Practitioners of oral history should follow the 30-year rule in relation to confidentiality that we also have for the release of state papers,' he told me. 'Academic historians do not generally approach the confidential sources issue in a way that journalists do for an obvious reason; they are rarely dealing with pressing matters of contemporary concern, nor should they be.' Ferriter makes the distinction between history and current affairs, adding that the interviewees are talking about people who are still alive. Commenting on oral history itself he said: 'Alongside the great opportunities it provides to talk directly to participants, it also raises issues of memory, skewed memory, agendas, settling of scores, etc.'

While the Belfast Project might be an extreme case for the oral historian – not many involve murder investigations – the academic community is still watching quietly in the wings. There is the obvious fear of sources drying up, but also that both historians and social scientists are looking at increasingly controversial subject matter, some of it illegal and some of it relating to international relations, or terrorism. Academics fear certain types of research will become impossible if they are perceived as an arm of the police, asking questions, interviewing people for that work to be then handed to the authorities. They, like journalists, want to be able to research, in the public interest, offering confidentiality where appropriate, if that means better research, with better information eventually making its way into the public domain. Whatever the outcome for the Belfast Project it is likely to have a profound impact on the growing area of oral history and probably social science research generally. ❐

©Michael Foley
41(3): 83/88
DOI: 10.1177/0306422012456133
www.indexoncensorship.org

Michael Foley lectures in journalism at the Dublin Institute of Technology and was formerly a journalist with the *Irish Times*

Index on Censorship

Celebrating **40 years of the world's best authors, artists and thinkers**

As the world's most influential free expression magazine, Index on Censorship is a must read for free thinkers everywhere. For 40 years, it has reported on free expression violations, published banned writing and given a voice to those who have been prevented from speaking out.

From freedom of information and state control of the internet to whistleblowing and jokes on Twitter, free expression is one of today's most challenging issues and something that affects us all. Through challenging and intelligent analysis, Index on Censorship sets the agenda for the most urgent free expression issues of the day.

Take advantage of our 40% discount on print subscriptions to celebrate 40 years of Index in Censorship

Margaret Atwood Isaac Babel Daniel Barenboim
Samuel Beckett Mikhail Bulgakov William Boyd
Noam Chomsky Ariel Dorfman Shirin Ebadi
Umberto Eco Harold Evans Nadine Gordimer

www.indexoncensorship.org/subscribe

El Salvador

Miguel Angel Parada

Keeping the university alive

The campus was shut down with the loss of 22 lives. The death squads are murdering students or teachers at the rate of one a week; yet 17,000 students are still being taught

Miguel Angel Parada, the rector of El Salvador's national university, visited London at the end of 1983 as part of an international tour to increase awareness of the plight of his university and of education at all levels in El Salvador. The university campus was occupied by the army on 26 June 1980, when 22 people were killed. They are still there, even after a government decree stipulating that it should be returned to the university authorities. Despite the occupation, Dr Parada and his colleagues offer courses to 17,000 students in rented premises throughout the city of El Salvador. Dr Parada's own position is particularly hazardous. His predecessor, Félix Ulloa Martínez, was murdered. He himself was arrested in 1981 when troops burst into a university administrative meeting and detained 20 members of the council. The kidnapping and murder of students and university teachers has continued unabated through 1983 (see box), the latest victim being Dr Enelson Escobar, a lecturer in the Faculty of Law, whose tortured body was found on 8 December 1983. His name, like that of Dr Parada, was on a list published by the Ejercito Secreto Anticomunista (ESA, the 'Secret Anti-Communist Army') of people with 'subversive connections'. In spite of the dangers, likely to increase still further as the March 1984 elections approach, Dr Parada remains outspoken in his defence of the university as the promoter of education in its widest sense, and the 'defender of rational, critical thought in a country turned over to barbarism'.

INDEX: What is the present situation in the university?

M. A. PARADA: Well, as you know, we have not been able to use our campus since June 1980. The soldiers have let us in to get some files and documents, but many more were destroyed. Even so, we try to run as many courses as we can in places we rent.

When they took over the university we were just leaving the first half of the academic year 1980, and in consequence of

UNDER SIEGE

During the civil war in El Salvador, academics and students were arrested, kidnapped and murdered. **Miguel Angel Parada** spoke to *Index* about surviving under extreme pressure

Miguel Angel Parada, the rector of El Salvador's national university, visited London at the end of 1983 as part of an international tour to increase awareness of the plight of his university and of education at all levels in El Salvador. It was the third year of a brutal 12-year civil war. The university campus was occupied by the army on 26 June 1980, when 22 people were killed. Despite the occupation, Dr Parada and his colleagues offered courses to 17,000 students in rented premises throughout the city of El Salvador. Dr Parada's own position was particularly hazardous. His predecessor, Felix Ulloa Martinez, was murdered. He himself was arrested in 1981 when troops burst into a university administrative meeting and detained 20 members of the council. The kidnapping and murder of students and university teachers continued unabated through 1983, the victims including Dr Enelson Escobar, a lecturer in the Faculty of Law, whose tortured body was found on 8 December 1983. His name, like that of Dr Parada, was on a list published by the Ejercito Secreto Anticomunista (ESA, the 'Secret Anti-Communist Army') of people with 'subversive connections'. In spite of the dangers, Dr Parada remained outspoken in his defence of the university as the promoter of education in its widest sense, and the 'defender of rational, critical thought in a country turned over to barbarism'.

Index: What is the present situation in the university?

Miguel Angel Parada: Well, as you know, we have not been able to use our campus since June 1980. The soldiers have let us in to get some files and documents, but many more were destroyed. Even so, we try to run as many courses as we can in places we rent.

When they took over the university we were just finishing the first half of the academic year 1980, with 30,000 students. It was only in 1982 that we could finish that academic year: but student numbers had dropped to 6,000. What happened to the rest? 24,000 young people who had wanted to study had been frightened away or

CARTA ABIERTA

A LAS PERSONAS QUE HAN PRIVADO DE SU LIBERTAD A NUESTRO PADRE Y ESPOSO LIC. HUGO FRANCISCO CARRILLO, JEFE DEL DEPARTAMENTO DE RELACIONES INTERNACIONALES DE LA FACULTAD DE JURISPRUDENCIA Y CIENCIAS SOCIALES DE LA UNIVERSIDAD DE EL SALVADOR, LES SUPLICAMOS E IMPLORAMOS RESPETARLE SU VIDA Y EN CASO LE IMPUTEN PARTICIPACION EN ACTIVIDADES FUERA DE LA LEY, PONERLO A DISPOSICION DE LOS TRIBUNALES O AUTORIDADES CORRESPONDIENTES PARA SU JUZGAMIENTO.

APELAMOS A DICHAS PERSONAS, PARA QUE NOS PROPORCIONEN NOTICIAS SOBRE LA SITUACION DE NUESTRO QUERIDO PADRE Y ESPOSO, POR CUALQUIER CANAL QUE LES SEA CONVENIENTE, A FIN DE TRAER UN POCO DE TRANQUILIDAD A NUESTRO HOGAR, QUE DESDE EL 14 DE SEPTIEMBRE DEL CORRIENTE AÑO, ESTA EN CONSTANTE ZOZOBRA POR SU AUSENCIA, SEÑORES MI ESPOSO PUEDE SER TODO, MENOS VIOLADOR DE LAS LEYES DIVINAS Y HUMANAS. JUNTO A EL TODO CAMINABA BIEN, AUNQUE SABIAMOS QUE LA TORMENTA AZOTABA A LA UNIVERSIDAD. ERAMOS ALGO ASI COMO UNA RESIGNADA PAREJA QUE ESPERA QUE PASE EL TEMPORAL, HOY LLUEVE EN MI ALMA Y SE CAYO EL ALERO EN EL QUE ME GUARECIA Y NO SE QUE HACER CUANDO MIS HIJOS ME PREGUNTAN POR SU PADRE.

POR MI, POR MIS HIJOS; POR LOS PADRES DE HUGO, ENTREGUENMELO CON VIDA, SANO Y SALVO.

POR FAVOR, QUEREMOS SABER DONDE ESTA, YA NO PODEMOS MAS CON ESTA ANGUSTIA DE NO SABER NADA DE EL.

SU ESPOSA: ALMA EVELYN DE CARRILLO
SUS HIJOS: HUGO RODRIGO, DE 6 AÑOS DE EDAD
FRANCISCO JOSE, DE 5 AÑOS
CAMILO FERNANDO, DE 3 AÑOS

TELEFONO: 26—5500

SAN SALVADOR, 10 DE OCTUBRE DE 1983.

forced to start work without qualifications. No country can afford to waste its future like that, especially not one like El Salvador, where there are so few professionals.

What reasons have the government given for the armed intervention?

The government claimed that the university was trying to operate as a state within a state, and not obeying the rule of law, but that is nonsense. The police or military could always have access to our campus, but only if they did so in the proper legal fashion. They – not us – were the ones who ignored our country's laws by bursting in violently and killing innocent people.

Then of course they said that we were a centre of subversion, a support base for the guerrillas. But in 1982 we pointed out to the Ministry of Education that the guerrillas seemed to be getting stronger and stronger, whereas we had been closed for two years – so how could we have been such an important base for them? These of course were just excuses, not the real reasons.

What were these then?

Historically, there has always been a great deal of tension between the government – in El Salvador as in many other Latin American countries – and the state universities. This is because in the universities people still try to think, still have ideals, and try to propose new ideas and models for society. They are continually faced with governments who do not believe in thinking, merely in repression. They cannot tolerate any criticism, anyone who denounces human rights violations or the abuse of power, or spotlights institutional injustice. The government and the university in El Salvador have never been allied, there has always been a contradiction between their efforts. This has always been the case, almost since 1841 when both the state of El Salvador and its university were established. And as the social conflict in our country has got worse, so have relations between government and university.

The government itself has stated publicly that the conflict in El Salvador is due to 50 years of neglect, corruption, and unrepresentative governments, so why blame the university? How in the midst of all this social turmoil can they expect the university to stay like an island of calm? The university is bound to reflect all the tensions and debates as to the rights and wrongs of the question.

The government said we were subversive, and pointed to the political graffiti all over the university walls. We replied that they should take a look at any wall in the city of El Salvador, and they would find exactly the same slogans. And if the armed forces, with all their troops, tanks, and helicopters, could not put a stop to it, how did they expect us to do so?

They also objected to the policy the university has of actively favouring those students with scant financial resources. Over the past 20 years we have made a

From Index on Censorship, 1984. An open letter to kidnappers of Hugo Francisco Carrillo from his family

conscious effort to recruit poorer students and to make sure that they are not kept from finishing their studies because of money problems. We have offered not only grants but small stipends to those most in need, as well as running university residences and restaurants, selling text books cheaply, and so on.

We argue that the right to education is a basic one, and that it is our responsibility therefore to give preference to those who might be denied that right for financial reasons; but the government also sees that as subversive.

How do you manage to continue?

It is getting more and more difficult. Our budget has been cut by almost 70 per cent over the past four years, and even without taking the extra expense of having to hire rooms into account, we do not have enough money to pay our staff.

We have lost about a quarter of our teachers. In the past few years, as many as 26 private universities have sprung up, some of them with more money and thus able to pay much better salaries. And of course, apart from those who drift away or prefer to go abroad, you must not forget that an average of one student or lecturer per week is being murdered in El Salvador.

The latest case, which happened now while I am out of the country, is the murder of Dr Enelson Escobar, a lecturer in the international relations department of the Faculty of Law. He was an economist who had always worked for the government, had even served abroad as a diplomat. But when he wanted to give the benefits of his experience by teaching in the university, he was kidnapped and killed by a right-wing death squad. They have apparently published leaflets accusing him of being a traitor to the country, of being in the university in order to pass government secrets to the guerrillas, but anyone who knows him knows that is absurd. To these people, the mere fact that he wanted to work in the university made him suspect, whatever his record or personal views.

Soon after your return to El Salvador there is not only the start of a new academic year but also elections in the country. What prospects do you see for the university in the coming months?

We are expecting more than 20,000 students to enrol for the academic year starting in February 1984, which shows how great the need is for the university.

But the pressures on us have become so intense, and are bound to get even worse in these pre-election months, that we are seriously wondering if it is worth the price we pay to carry on. The fact that we give lectures in the same place and at the same time each day makes us sitting targets for the death squads. There have already been paid advertisements in some newspapers with lists of students and teachers supposed to be 'subversives' – these are little more than an invitation to kill.

One plan we are discussing is for the whole university staff to go into exile and denounce the government, showing it is impossible in El Salvador today to have any university education. We do not expect anything very much from the elections themselves. It seems to me that if the government and the armed forces consider something like the university as a threat, when we make no political claims at all and have absolutely no wish to compete for political power, then any opposition party which does want to dispute political supremacy with them can have no guarantees whatsoever. In such circumstances, who can believe that the elections will be free and peaceful, or that the results will be respected if they go against the government? ☐

©Miguel Angel Parada
41(3): 90/95
DOI: 10.1177/0306422012456137
www.indexoncensorship.org

CREATIONISM BY STEALTH

Campaigners are using new tactics to bring their doctrine into the classroom. **Heather L Weaver** reports on attempts to undermine the teaching of evolution

Last April, Tennessee became the second state to pass a law that prohibits public schools from restraining teachers who disregard state-mandated science curricula by instructing students about alleged 'weaknesses' and critiques of the scientific theory of evolution. Enacted under the guise of safeguarding academic freedom, the law purports to protect teachers 'from discipline for teaching scientific subjects in an objective manner'. In reality, it gives cover to teachers who want to undercut scientifically accurate lessons about evolution by injecting veiled creationist doctrine into science classes.

This new focus on 'academic freedom' is just the latest tactic employed by a decades-long, surprisingly adaptable creationism movement, which aims to undermine, to the greatest extent possible, the teaching of evolution in US public schools. Blaming modern scientific developments – including the widespread acceptance of evolution – for destroying man's reverence of God and giving birth to moral relativism, creationists' first salvo in the fight against evolution was to criminalise its instruction by public school teachers.

Tennessee's Butler Act, passed in 1925, was perhaps the most infamous of these efforts, prohibiting the teaching of 'any theory that denies the Story of the Divine Creation of man as taught in the Bible' or any theory 'that man has descended from a lower order of animals'. Violators could be charged with a misdemeanor and fined up to $500. When high school biology teacher John T Scopes was prosecuted under the law, famed attorney Clarence Darrow and the American Civil Liberties Union (ACLU), then a new organisation formed to protect individual rights and liberties, stepped up to represent him. The ensuing 'Scopes Monkey Trial' drew derision from around the country and the world, Tennessee became an international laughing stock, and the Butler Act was eventually repealed.

Despite the debacle that was the Scopes Monkey Trial, however, it was hardly the end of the creationism movement. Although teachers were no longer hauled into court and prosecuted as criminals, states continued to outlaw the teaching of evolution in public schools until the late 1960s, when the US supreme court struck down an Arkansas ban. Explaining that the sole purpose of the Arkansas law was to 'suppress the teaching of a theory which, it was thought, "denied" the divine creation of man', the court reasoned that allowing the state 'to blot out a particular theory because of its supposed conflict with the biblical account, literally read' would infringe the separation of church and state guaranteed by the US constitution.

Undeterred, creationists marched on, taking a new tack. If they could not ban outright the teaching of evolution, they decided they would at least curtail it by permitting evolution instruction only where creationism was afforded 'equal time' alongside it. But that strategy also met its demise at the supreme court, which, in 1987, overturned Louisiana's 'Balanced Treatment for Creation-Science and Evolution-Science in Public School Instruction Act'. The court explained that, 'by requiring either the banishment of the theory of evolution from public school classrooms or the presentation of a religious viewpoint that rejects evolution in its entirety', the statute improperly 'employ[ed] the symbolic and financial support of government to achieve a religious purpose'.

After a second devastating loss in the nation's highest court, creationists should have been ready to pack it in. Indeed, the supreme court had made it abundantly clear that any effort to *proscribe* evolution instruction or *prescribe* the teaching of creationism in public schools would never gain legal traction. Yet, it appears that one throwaway line in that 1987 decision, which reserved judgment on potential laws 'requir[ing] that scientific critiques of prevailing scientific theories be taught', gave them hope.

Seizing on this language, creationists set out to develop a comprehensive, biblically-based scientific theory that would uncover the weaknesses of evolution and could be taught in public schools. That theory, 'intelligent

ACLU lawyer Clarence Darrow defends John Scopes, who was accused of teaching evolution in a Tennessee high school, 10 July 1925
Credit: The Art Archive/Alamy

design', posited that nature is so irreducibly complex that it could only have been created by an 'intelligent designer'. But they could not produce an iota of credible scientific evidence in support of the claim. As a result, the crusade to integrate intelligent design into public school science curricula quickly stalled after a federal court ruled that it was religious doctrine that merely repackaged creationist beliefs into pseudo-scientific terms.

Reeling from loss after loss in the courts, it is not surprising that creationism advocates began to construct a new narrative: they started casting themselves as victims, subjected to decades of persecution and discrimination in the academic world because of their religious beliefs. And, also not surprisingly, soon after, they began to peddle the antidote to their alleged oppression – legislation, such as the Tennessee law, that promised to protect the academic freedom of those who question evolution and ensure that students receive all information necessary to think critically about the matter.

Although these laws are carefully worded to avoid references to the Bible, creationism and intelligent design, make no mistake: they pose a serious threat both to science education and the separation of church and state, which is a fundamental founding principle and mandated by the First Amendment to the US constitution. Indeed, the academic freedom laws advanced by creationist groups are so dangerous precisely because they are so insidious. As watchdog organisations like the National Center for Science Education and the ACLU have warned, these academic freedom laws are nothing more than 'stealth creationism'.

For example, after proclaiming that instruction in some scientific subjects, such as 'biological evolution' and 'the chemical origins of life', may prove controversial or cause 'debate and disputation', the Tennessee law provides that officials may not prohibit any teacher 'from helping students understand, analyse, critique, and review in an objective manner the scientific strengths and scientific weaknesses of existing scientific theories'. It may sound benign enough, but this language has been carefully cultivated by creationism advocates to suggest, first and foremost, that there is debate in the scientific community about evolution's soundness as a scientific theory and, second, that this controversy makes sense because evolution is plagued by a series of purported 'weaknesses'.

In fact, within the legitimate scientific community, there is no controversy over the validity of evolution as a scientific theory. And the 'weaknesses' that proponents of the bill hope teachers will discuss are recycled intelligent design claims, unsupported by scientific evidence and resoundingly rejected by scientists.

Still, pressured by creationist groups and extreme religious factions, lawmakers across the country continue to propose 'academic freedom' measures each year. Most have failed to make it through the state legislatures. But with the passage of the Louisiana Science Education Act and the recent victory in Tennessee, concerns are rising. While watchdog groups, such as the ACLU, are closely monitoring these statutes and building cases to challenge them in court, the laws are written in a way that purposefully obfuscates their true aim and likely effect and are, therefore, harder to challenge on their face than past anti-evolution statutes.

In the meantime, these stealthy tactics may very well prove successful. A study published last year by *Science* indicated that only 28 per cent of US public high school biology teachers provide adequate instruction in evolution. According to the study, hoping to avoid a backlash from students and parents, many teachers simply 'fail to explain the nature of scientific inquiry, undermine the authority of established experts, and legitimise creationist arguments'. Laws encouraging and authorising teachers to spread misinformation about evolution will only exacerbate this problem by emboldening those teachers already prone to teaching creationist beliefs and engendering a more difficult and politically charged environment for those who seek to abide by state science curricula.

In spite of creationists' claims of martyrdom, discouraging and undermining the transmission of accurate scientific information in this manner is entirely irreconcilable with basic academic freedom principles. It turns academic freedom on its head, transforming it from a shield against censorship into a sword of suppression.

The truth is that advocates of these laws are not interested in protecting academic freedom or critical thinking. Rather, by wrapping anti-evolution measures in these traditionally venerated values, creationists hope to silence potential critics. Many who might have otherwise scrutinised the law are disarmed, lulled into a false sense of security. After all, what could be bad about a law that aims to bolster academic freedom and critical thinking? Meanwhile, even lawmakers and others who recognise that these laws promote stealth creationism may be reluctant to object because they do not want to be painted as opponents of these noble principles.

In light of these obstacles, it is imperative that educators and activists fighting laws like the Tennessee statute aim first to strip away the cloak of academic freedom and reveal these laws for what they really are – wolves in sheep's clothing. Of course, even assuming we succeed in staving off this latest attack, if history is any indication, creationism advocates will adapt and quickly find new ways to undermine the teaching of evolution in public schools. That's the funny thing about the creationism movement: it's always evolving. ❑

©Heather L Weaver
41(3): 98/102
DOI: 10.1177/0306422012457491
www.indexoncensorship.org

Heather L Weaver is a staff attorney for the American Civil Liberties Union programme on Freedom of Religion and Belief

ROYAL CHILL

Insulting the king is a matter of national security in Thailand. **Sinfah Tunsarawuth** reports on a campaign to protect free speech

On 29 February, Worachet Pakeerut, a star lecturer in law, was assaulted in broad daylight on his own university campus. Two young brothers punched him in the face before speeding off on a motorcycle. Worachet is a well-known public figure in Thailand: a brilliant academic who has challenged higher court decisions on the country's laws and constitution. So news of the incident was reported on Thai television and pictures of Worachet's bruised cheeks were on the front pages of all major Thai dailies.

The two men turned themselves in at the police station the next morning and announced that they disagreed with Worachet's campaign to amend Thailand's strict lèse majesté law, which makes it illegal to insult King Bhumibol Adulyadej and his family members. A week later, a Bangkok court sentenced them to three months' imprisonment.

Worachet has angered many people in Thailand. In March last year, he led a band of young law lecturers at Thammasat University, known as the Nitirat group, which announced an elaborate and wide-ranging proposal to amend Section 112 of the penal code: anybody who 'defames, insults or threatens the king, the queen, the heir-apparent or the regent' can be

subject to imprisonment for three to 15 years. Many hardcore royalists see his campaign as an effort to dissolve the country's monarchy.

Lèse majesté is currently a crime against national security; anyone can accuse another person of the offence. The chill on free speech has also been a concern for foreign governments and international human rights organisations, as there are fears that political rivals use the law to silence and harass their opponents.

The issue has also been at the heart of power politics in Thailand since the overthrow of Prime Minister Thaksin Shinawatra in 2006: military leaders disliked him for his anti-royalist position. His supporters, the red shirts, are calling for him to return from exile. Anti-Thaksin protesters have said they would challenge any move to amend the lèse majesté law.

Prosecutions soared after the country's 2006 military coup

Nitirat argues that Section 112 should be re-categorised: currently it falls under national security legislation, but the group asserts that it should be reclassified as an offence that relates to the 'reputation of the king, the queen, the heir-apparent and the regent', offences that are not serious enough to 'affect the existence of integrity and security of the kingdom'. The maximum jail term should be reduced to three years. The law should not stipulate a minimum jail term as Section 112 does. Without a minimum term, the court could exercise its discretion as it sees fit. Furthermore, Nitirat proposes that the penalty for defaming the queen, the heir-apparent or the regent should be less severe than the penalty for defaming the king, as he commands a higher status. Adopting the amendments, Nitirat argues, will ensure the law complies with the principle of proportionality, whereby the penalty of an offence should be proportionate to its severity, in line with international standards and Thailand's own constitution. In cases where the defendant can prove the statement is true, he or she should not be penalised.

Bolder still, Nitirat asserts that there should be circumstances for pardoning such offences. The group argues that a person should be found not guilty of defaming the monarchy if he or she criticises or expresses an

Worachet Pakeerut after he was attacked at Thammasat University,
Bangkok, 29 February 2012
Credit: AP Photo

opinion 'in good faith for the protection of a government under a democratic system with the monarch as the head of state under the constitution and for the protection of the constitution in serving academic or public interest'.

Nitirat also proposes that the current lèse majesté law should be amended so that only the Office of His Majesty's Principal Private Secretary can file a complaint. This would certainly keep the number of prosecutions down, which soared following Thailand's September 2006 military coup.

In January, Worachet's campaign gathered further momentum after other academics, writers, artists and members of the general public signed up to form the Campaign Committee for the Amendment of Section 112. The committee launched its first major public meeting on 15 January at Thammasat University, which was attended by many members of the red shirts, supporters of former Prime Minister Thaksin.

At the meeting, Worachet explained Nitirat's proposals and launched a petition. The plan was to collect at least 10,000 signatures to enable the submission to parliament of a proposed draft for amendments to the law.

However, it turned out to be the first and last gathering at the university. The rector, Professor Somkid Lertpaitoon, announced that he would no longer allow Nitirat or the committee to organise any activity on campus that could be seen as a 'political movement'. In a television interview with Somkid, the rector said that the group should not hold any activity that could 'affect or instigate social conflict'. Worachet was interviewed in the same broadcast and was bombarded with criticism in the royalist press. It's worth noting that student uprisings took place on the Thammasat campus in the 1970s, and a number of students were killed by the military. Many were accused of being against the monarchy.

In response to the rector's objections, Worachet declared that his own university had restricted his academic freedom and denied that he had launched a political movement, stating that he was not associated with any party: people gathered in seeking an amendment to a law should not be seen as political.

He added that the university should allow all parties to discuss the proposed amendments to Section 112 in order to find out whether Thai society wanted to adopt them. If Thai people don't exercise reason when talking to each other, he said, 'then when will we become a "democratic civilization?"'

In late May, key members of the campaign led a march of a few hundred people to submit a draft amendment based on Nitirat's blueprint to parliament, along with 26,968 signatures of support.

Parliament will now scrutinise the authenticity and legitimacy of the signatories before it potentially starts the process of turning it into law. However, the current government, run by Prime Minister Yingluck Shinawatra, a younger sister of Thaksin, has said it will not take the initiative to amend the lèse majesté law, which could slow down, if not obstruct, the process.

Since the beginning of the year, there have been few reports of new lèse majesté cases and the authorities do not seem to have been very enthusiastic in pursuing some of those pending. So it's possible that Worachet's campaign for reform may already be having an effect. ❐

©Sinfah Tunsarawuth
41(3): 103/107
DOI: 10.1177/0306422012456809
www.indexoncensorship.org

Sinfah Tunsarawuth is an independent media lawyer and writer based in Bangkok. He can be reached at sinfah@hotmail.com

A censorship chronicle incorporating academic freedom stories from Agence France Presse (AFP), BBC, Chronicle of Higher Education, *Guardian*, Index on Censorship, Knight Center for Journalism, Network for Education & Academic Rights (Near), Radio Free Europe/Radio Liberty (RFE/RL), Reporters sans frontières (RSF), Southeast Asian Press Alliance (Seapa), *Times of India*, Voice of America and other organisations affiliated with the International Freedom of Expression Exchange (IFEX)

Azerbaijan

Professor **Rafiq Aliyev** was demoted on 7 November 2011 after speaking out about the case of imprisoned activist and blogger Bakhtiyar Hajiyev. Aliyev, who gave an interview on 1 November about the unjust imprisonment of the activist, was stripped of his chairmanship of a robotics research group at the Oil Academy. (RFE/RL)

Bahrain

In May 2012, a letter from human rights activist and teacher **Mahdi Abu Deeb** to the king of Bahrain was smuggled out of Abu Deeb's prison cell. The president of the Bahrain Teachers' Association was arrested in April 2011 for taking part in pro-democracy protests. Charged with 10 years' imprisonment for 'halting the education process' and 'attempting to overthrow the regime by force', his letter called for the king to honour human rights. There were reports that Abu Deeb had been tortured while in prison. (Human Rights First)

Jaleela al Salman was released on 1 November 2011. The vice president of the Bahrain Teachers' Association was arrested on 18 October 2011 without a warrant. On 25 September, a military court sentenced her to three years in prison on charges of 'inciting hatred towards the regime', 'calling for a teachers' strike', and 'attempting to overthrow the ruling system by force'. Al Salman was initially detained from 29 March to 21 August after going on hunger strike and has been outspoken about the state of human rights in the country. (Bahrain Center for Human Rights, Index on Censorship)

About **63 students** who actively supported the protest movement in 2011 were notified that they had been expelled at the beginning of the autumn academic term. Despite a statement from the king saying many of them should be reinstated, officials at Bahrain Polytechnic refused to reinstate many of the dismissed students. Several were penalised for posting comments on social network sites. Some students reported that when they returned to university, they were asked to sign new code of conduct forms, agreeing to not take part in political activities. (Chronicle of Higher Education, Index on Censorship, Voice of America)

Chad

Two students were detained for organising protests in May 2011. **Bebkika Passoua Alexis** and **Nedoumbayel Nekaou** were accused of possessing documents urging Chadians to take part in pro-democracy protests inspired by events in Tunisia and Egypt. There were allegations that the students had been tortured while in prison. Their trial had been postponed three times because security officials failed to appear in court. (Amnesty International)

China

Authorities instructed the Beijing Institute of Technology to cancel **inter-university debates** scheduled to take place on 9 April 2011. The event was planned to coincide with the anniversary of the 1911 revolution, which marked the beginning of the demise of the Manchu dynasty. Sixteen universities were due to take part in the debates, which were organised by the Communist Youth League of Beijing. The move followed a spate of arrests in the wake of calls for Arab spring-inspired protests. (Near)

Cyprus

A former university rector accused authorities from the city of Famagusta of censorship after his lecture about an explosion at a naval facility was cancelled. **Stavros Zenios**, who was informed of the cancellation on 13 October 2011, spoke on the same subject in Larnaca on 12 October. (About Larnaca)

Dominican Republic

In February 2012, the Dominican Journalism Guild proposed a law that would require mandatory membership for all **journalists**. Under the law, those working without accreditation from an approved journalism course or relevant undergraduate degree would face penalties and possible prison sentences. The Inter American Press Association declared the move unconstitutional, stating that all citizens have the right to disseminate information. (Knight Center for Journalism)

Egypt

The screening of award-winning Iranian film *A Separation* was cancelled on 8 March 2012. The board of administration at Cairo University's Faculty of Pharmacy revoked the screening licence after fundamentalist groups at the university complained that the film promotes secularism, Shiism and supports Bashar al Assad's regime in Syria. (Arabic Network for Human Rights Information)

India

The government announced in May 2012 that plans were under way to create an academic council or institute that would rule on **textbook content**. The move followed uproar over a cartoon published in a politics studies textbook, depicting iconic Dalit leader BR Ambekdar in a negative light. On 15 May 2012, education minister Kapil Sibal called for the cartoon to be removed and questioned the validity of including cartoons in textbooks. (BBC, *Times of India*)

Jadavpur University professor **Ambikesh Mahapatra** was arrested on 13 April 2012, accused of circulating cartoons that mocked West Bengal's chief minister. (*Hindustan Times, Times of India*)

Iran

Graduate student **Omid Kokabee** was sentenced to 10 years' imprisonment on 13 May 2012. The physics student was found guilty of conspiring with Israel against Iran. He had studied in Spain and the United States but frequently travelled back to Iran, particularly over the course of 2010. Kokabee had been detained without trial since February 2011. (Nature)

Setareh Elyasi was expelled from the University of Cultural Heritage in December 2011. University authorities accused Elyasi of causing disorder and had warned her to discontinue

any student activism. She had been waiting for her diploma to be issued for two years. (International Campaign for Human Rights in Iran)

Seven Baha'i lecturers were found guilty of membership to a 'deviant sect' and of 'taking action against the security of the country' in November 2011. **Vahid Mahmoud** and **Kamran Mortezaie** were given sentences of five years' imprisonment and four-year terms were handed down to **Mahmoud Badavam, Nooshin Khadem, Farhad Sedghi, Riaz Sobhani** and **Ramin Zibaie**. The academics, who are affiliated with the Baha'i Institute for Higher Education, were originally detained in June 2011. (Iran Press Watch)

Political science student **Peyman Aref** was punished with 74 lashes for insulting President Ahmadinejad on 9 October 2011. Aref was arrested in the aftermath of the 2009 disputed election and sentenced in March 2010. He was also charged with insulting the president after he wrote a letter to Ahmadinejad, criticising the government's treatment of student protesters during the elections. (Guardian)

In September 2011, a judge ruled that prominent student activist **Majid Tavakoli** will be banned from studying at any of the country's universities upon his release from prison. Tavakoli is serving an eight-and-a-half year jail sentence for a range of convictions, including insulting the country's establishment. He was arrested at a student gathering at Amir Kabir University in 2009. (RFE/RL)

The spokesman for an Iranian reformist student organisation **Abdollah Momeni** was refused medical leave from Evin Prison on

12 July 2011. Momeni was arrested in 2009 following the contested presidential election. Medical care was thought to have been denied because Momeni wrote an open letter to Aytollah Khamenei about his treatment in prison. (Near)

Israel

Tel Aviv University asked lecturers to report on **students who organised a demonstration** in December 2011. The university requested faculty members in the philosophy, literature and history departments to view a YouTube video showing students encouraging their peers to take part in protests and identify students with whom they were familiar. The university stated that protest was illegal on campus if not authorised. (Ha'aretz)

Malaysia

Demonstrators at a university in Kuala Lumpur were attacked and detained on 1 January 2012. **Students from Sultan Idris University** were calling for academic freedom and demonstrating in support of Adam Adli, a student who was criticised and threatened with violence for removing a flag bearing a photograph of the prime minister from the headquarters of the United Malays National Organisation, one of the country's major political parties. (Malaysian Insider)

Student **Adam Adli** received threats and was repeatedly harassed after he replaced a flag bearing the president's face with a flag calling for academic freedom on 17 December 2011. Adam Adli lowered the flag during a demonstration against the government's proposed amendments to the country's Universities and University Colleges Act, which students say impacts on their free expression. Adli's family were also thought to have been harassed. The Universiti Pendidikan Sultran Idris student issued a statement to the press, claiming that a plainclothes policeman had been among those who had intimidated him. (Free Malaysia Today)

An appeal court ruled on 30 October 2011 that it was unconstitutional to prohibit students from political activities. **University students** launched a campaign calling for the 1971 Universities and University Colleges Act to be repealed and filed a lawsuit against the International University of Malaysia in 2010 after being threatened with legal action for political campaigning. Charges against them were dropped. (AFP)

Mauritius

The ministry of education announced that it was considering cancelling some **courses at the University of Mauritius**. Anthropology, history, international affairs and political sciences were among the areas of research affected by the proposals. Ministry officials claimed the subjects did not offer students enough job prospects. (University World News)

Palestine

On 2 April 2012, Israeli security forces raided **Quds Net News Agency**, a newly-launched media centre in East Jerusalem, set up by al Quds University. The raid took place on the same day the community radio, television and online network organised a ceremony to launch the services. (RSF)

South Africa

University professors criticised the Protection of Information Act on 18 December 2011, arguing that the legislation threatens academic freedom. It will particularly affect research focusing on **security issues, legal research into classified documents and government transparency**, according to academics. The act was passed on 22 November 2011. (University World News, World Association of Newspapers and News Publishers)

South Korea

The Ministry of Education, Science and Technology issued a list of **educational institutions** banned from admitting foreign students at the beginning of January 2012. The move followed a four-month investigation into hundreds of educational facilities, 200 of them universities, conducted by a committee tasked with restructuring higher education. The committee was set up after students protested in June 2012, demanding lower tuition fees. The government stated that the restructuring was part of plans to improve higher education ahead of the next presidential election. (CS Monitor, University World News)

Syria

Nuclear physics professor **Ous Abdel Karim Khalil** was shot and killed in Homs on 28 September 2011. In the same week, the deputy rector in the architecture department at al-Ba'ath University, **Mohamed Ali Aqil**, and **Nael Dakhi**, who taught at a petrochemical institute, were killed. Activists regarded the murders as a renewed attack against the scientific community in Syria, which had been targeted in the 1980s. Opposition politicians claimed that up to 10 academics had been killed in September, most of them in Homs. There were also reports that more than **70 students** from universities

in Damascus, Homs and Aleppo had been arrested for taking part in protests. (Ahram Online, BBC, University World News)

Thailand

Blogger **Norawase Yospiyasathien** was arrested on lèse majesté charges on 5 August 2011. The arrest came after the deputy rector at Kasetsart University filed a suit against the graduate, whose blogposts were published during the last year of his degree and were deemed to be insulting to the monarchy. The rector said he had been pressured by the university council to press charges against him in order to protect the university's reputation. Yospiyasathien was released on bail on 10 August. He was thought to have been the youngest person arrested on lèse majesté charges. A campaign group highlighted the role of the rector in the arrest. (Seapa)

Togo

The government announced the temporary closure of two **universities** on 9 December 2011 following student protests over amendments to financial aid policies. Students reported that security forces used teargas to disperse crowds in Lome and Kara. (AFP)

Turkey

On 2 January 2012, police arrested **23 people** during a confrontation between nationalist and left-wing students at the Byazit campus of Istanbul University. Most of those arrested were members of the pro-Kurdish Peace and Democracy Party and the rest were members of other left-leaning parties. At least one journalist, who was covering the incident, was also arrested. (Bianet, *Hurriyet Daily News*)

A hundred members of an international network supporting academic freedom staged a demonstration on the opening day of the trial of **Büşra Ersanlı**, a political scientist at Marmara University in Istanbul. Ersanlı was arrested in October 2011 on terrorism charges. She is accused of supporting the Kurdistan Workers' Party. If convicted she faces up to 20 years in jail. Other academics, including epidemiologist Onur Hamzaoğlu, have also been targeted. (Nature, Voice of America)

United Kingdom

On 25 June 2012, as the trial was due to begin, London primary school Durand Academy dropped defamation charges against **Lambeth Council**. The academy had claimed the council's chief auditor had made a 'serious allegation of financial impropriety' when it requested information about Durand's management. Despite the case being dropped, taxpayers incurred substantial costs because both the claimant and defendant are state-funded bodies, a fact that libel reform campaigners said clearly illustrated the need for urgent change. (Index on Censorship)

Trinity School in Leamington banned a pupil from displaying a dress made of condoms as part of an art exhibition on 17 February 2012. The teenager, **Meg Todd**, created the dress for an exam project based on the theme 'contagion', but was told, along with another student who had incorporated condoms into her artwork, that it was not consistent with the Catholic school's ethos. (*Leamington Courier*)

On 16 November 2011, a tribunal ruled that universities must release information about controversial research, including animal testing. The ruling, which followed a law-suit filed by the British Union for the Abolition of Vivisection against Newcastle University, will mean that exemptions from freedom of information requests will become more difficult. The university claimed the decision could put scientists carrying out the research in danger. The president of the Royal Society called for the **Freedom of Information Act** to be reviewed, insisting that the legislation was being used to intimidate researchers. Newcastle University announced plans to appeal the decision. (*Independent, University World News*)

Counter-terrorism expert **Dr Rod Thornton** was suspended on 4 May 2011 after he published a critical report on academic freedom at Nottingham University, particularly looking at the treatment of one of its students and a former employee. The report, which was published on the British International Studies Association website, was taken down after alleged pressure from the university. It focused on the 2008 case of MA student Rizwaan Sabir and Nottingham University staff member Hicham Yezza, who were arrested and detained for six days under the Terrorism Act 2000 after they downloaded and printed three documents, among them 'The al Qaeda Training Manual', a publication that was in the public domain and is now stocked by Nottingham University's library. Thornton's report criticises the university for not carrying out a risk assessment before consulting police and accuses the university of stifling debate on the matter and silencing anyone who challenges the university's version of events. (*Guardian,* Index on Censorship)

United States

On 7 July 2012, a United States federal court ruled that recorded interviews forming part of a research project on the Irish Troubles should be handed over to the Police Service of Northern Ireland (PSNI). In May 2011, the PSNI took legal steps to seize parts of the Boston College Research Project's archive, material it argued would assist in an investigation into a 1972 murder. **Boston College**'s oral history project ran from 2001 to 2006, with the aim of collecting material that would build knowledge and understanding around the long-running violent and political conflict in Northern Ireland. It included interviews with both republican and loyalist activists, who were promised that their narratives would remain confidential. Researchers on the project have also appealed part of the lower court's decision, challenging its ruling that the oral histories genuinely cast enough light on the killing of Ms McConville to outweigh the threat posed to academic freedom. (BBC, Index on Censorship, Times Higher Education)

In May 2012, Tennessee became the second US state to protect the **academic freedom of teachers in public schools**. The new laws also stipulate that schools have a responsibility to respect opinions, encourage critical thinking and foster debate. Under the legislation, individual teachers are able to discuss the merits of creationism and question aspects of evolution, though changes to the curriculum cannot be instated. (Huffington Post)

In January 2012, an Arizona schools authority ordered the suspension of **Mexican-American Studies programmes** in a Tucson school district. The decision followed claims that the courses violated a controversial state law and resulted in the banning of several books, including *Critical Race Theory* by Richard Delgado and Jean Stefancic and *500 Years of Chicano History in Pictures* edited by Elizabeth Martinez. The ethnic studies courses were accused of promoting the 'overthrow of the United States government' and 'promoting resentment towards a race or class of people'. First Amendment campaigners and some of the authors of the banned books responded by launching the 'Librotraficante' movement, smuggling banned books and other books taught as part of the course into Tucson from neighbouring states. (Daily Beast, *Guardian*, Huffington Post)

Funding was withdrawn from school newspaper the **Beacon** following the publication of an article about premarital sex on 8 December 2011. The Student Council at Yeshiva University, an Orthodox Jewish college in New York, took the decision, sparking a campus-wide debate on censorship. (*Wall Street Journal*)

An advisory panel on biosecurity recommended that **research papers** on how to create a form of the H5N1 avian-influenza virus be partially censored in December 2011. Though the National Science Advisory was alerted to the dangers of the information being in the public domain by a disease expert and the move was largely supported by the authors of the research, the

decision raised concerns among some professionals about the ethics of withholding information that might be used to save lives. (Chronicle of Higher Education)

On 19 September 2011, ten students were prosecuted on charges of 'conspiring to disturb a meeting' and 'disturbing a meeting'. The **'Irvine 11'** were found guilty after they disrupted a speech delivered by Israeli ambassador Michael Oren at the University of California campus at Irvine. Charges against an 11th student involved in the February 2010 incident were dropped after the student agreed to community service as compensation. (Index on Censorship, *LA Times*)

An exhibition at Trinity College in Hartford, Connecticut, was first postponed and then cancelled on 14 September 2011 after college administrators claimed the artist used 'illegally obtained materials' in his work. Artist **Poster Boy**'s exhibition *'Street Alchemy'* included two altered billboards; the guerilla artist admitted that he had stolen raw materials to create his art. (*Harvard Courant*)

The American Civil Liberties Union (ACLU) filed a lawsuit against a Missouri school district after it blocked student access to lesbian,

gay, bisexual and transgender (LGBT) content on 16 August 2011. The ACLU filed the complaint on behalf of the Campus Pride organisation and other organisations that discovered their content had been blocked. The Camdentown school district used a filtering system that blocks hundreds of sites containing LGBT-related information, a move that the ACLU identified as unconstitutional. (QNotes)

A US district court heard the case of evangelical Christian **James Deferio** on 10 August 2011. He had attempted to preach on the campus of the State University of New York at Albany but was told he had to apply for a permit 30 days in advance and pay processing and facility rental fees, leading him to file a First Amendment lawsuit. The university rejected Deferio's application and announced that it was revising its policy for assessing applications the day before the hearing. Deferio has spoken on a number of US campuses, often displaying signs. The First Amendment provides for open debate in public places. The judge adjourned the hearing, requesting more thorough information from both sides. (**Huffington Post**)

Edited by Natasha Schmidt
DOI 10.1177/0306422012456827

COSTING LIVES

In many parts of the world, malaria experts are denied access to vital scientific publications. **Bart Knols** makes the case for open access 2.0

For most of us, it's entirely logical that medical practitioners should be familiar with the latest scientific knowledge and evidence-based practices in order to treat ailments. This forms our fundamental basis of trust in medical professionals. If your doctor suggests a CT scan or drug X, you follow that advice on the basis of trust. So how would you feel if your doctor confesses that he lacks the latest scientific information about your condition? That he can prescribe a drug but is not sure if it is the best treatment? Before long you would be consulting someone else. But what if you live in sub-Saharan Africa, where the vast majority of medical personnel, as well as scientists, researchers and medical students, remain badly deprived of the latest medical developments? Not because they lack access to the internet, but simply because they cannot afford to pay for access to information. This is the harsh reality today. Subscription paywalls make access to essential information impossible.

Malaria kills between 0.7 and 1.2 million people annually, mostly young children and pregnant women in Africa. Today, more than 800 million people live without the fear of malaria in countries where the risk of contracting the disease was once significant. This shows that it can be eliminated, perhaps even globally as happened with smallpox. But in the tropics, where malaria still reigns, nature remains way ahead of our efforts: parasites constantly evolve and develop resistance to curative drugs and mosquitoes do the same, making our meagre armature of insecticidal sprays laughable. And so a malaria industry has ensued, involving an estimated 8,000-10,000 scientists around the world, their research fuelled by millions of dollars from funding bodies and the search for new and creative ways to end this menace. From vaccines to novel drugs, from proteomics to anthropological fieldwork, from genetically-engineered mosquitoes to climate change effects, the malaria research machinery runs overtime, producing nine scientific articles every day. That's more than 3,000 new pieces of information each year, all in pursuit of solving the giant malaria puzzle.

One would assume that this volume of scientific insight would be visible in the real world of malaria control – but a closer look reveals a surprising truth. The controversial insecticide DDT continues to be sprayed in many developing countries, though it was banned in the USA and Europe in the 1970s because of environmental and health concerns. Alternatively, millions of African children are covered with mosquito nets, often coated with insecticides, as they sleep. Although these methods have saved countless lives, resistance to both DDT and pyrethroids, the insecticides used for net impregnation, is spreading across Africa at an unprecedented rate. But why, when the global scientific community produces more than 3,000 articles on malaria each year, are these older methods being so heavily relied on? A decade ago, when the three genomes of the malaria players (human, parasite and mosquito) became available, there was huge optimism that a whole new arsenal of tools would emerge. It didn't. Why is valorisation of new scientific information – the process of making knowledge useful for society at large – so painfully slow, if not absent?

A recent survey of malaria research articles published in 2010–11 showed that 48 per cent were open access and so could be read without payment. But that also means that every second article had restricted access, requiring some form of payment to access. Those working in well-endowed academic institutions in the north don't even notice this paywall in their day-to-day mining of scholarly material. But for scientists in the south this is crucial. If you can't afford to pay, you can't read. Another survey revealed that three-quarters of malaria professionals based in Africa and Asia often can't read beyond an article's abstract. Only two per cent never experience access problems. The net result is disparity in knowledge, which is a double

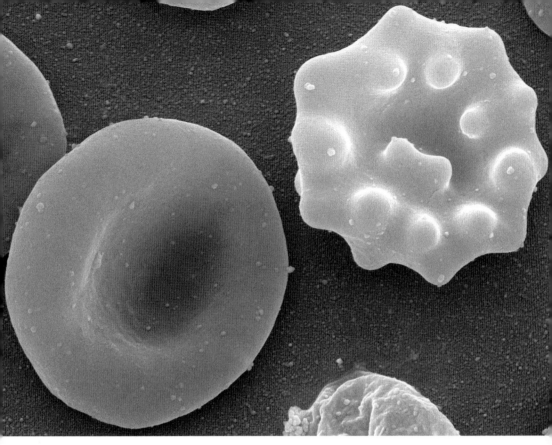

Malaria-infected red blood cell
Credit: Juergen Berger/Science Photo Library

whammy for southerners, as they live in countries where malaria kills daily. Taken one step further, this disparity can be seen as a prime reason why so few scientists from developing countries become global players in the public health arena. It is simply too hard for them to work on par with the West and on the forefront of scientific endeavour when always lagging behind in knowledge acquisition and utilisation.

Publishers argue that the HINARI Access to Research in Health Programme initiative, which they set up jointly with the World Health Organisation, provides free access to content for institutions in developing countries – but this only applies for as long as the GNI per capita remains below US$1,600 a year. That's tough for South Africa and Gabon, and recently even Bangladesh became too 'rich' and its free access threatened. Out of academics surveyed from Africa, South America and Asia, 41, 79, and 92 per cent respectively claimed never to use HINARI or were not even aware of its existence. Dr Peter Murray-Rust, a molecular informatics specialist at the University of Cambridge, claimed that HINARI 'is nothing more than the crumbs of charity' and that publishers don't give access to *their* content – it's *academics'* content that is given for free. It is certainly true that we scientists have been submissive to the oligopoly of academic publishers, which claims ownership of our work, often through transfer of copyright. By allowing it to be locked up behind paywalls, we have helped academic publishing to become one of the most profitable businesses today.

Because the lack of access to scientific research diminishes the communication of knowledge and creates disparities between those who have access and those who don't, effective application of new knowledge to ongoing research is hindered, as is much-needed change in policy for better malaria control in the field. And with scientific publishing having become the end point for research rather than the starting point for change in the real world, academics have come to grips with a system where lack of access to work no longer matters. 'Publish or perish' still dominates over 'publish for impact'.

And there's a further question to be asked: is it morally and ethically acceptable to run a business based on withholding information from those most in need of it? Do we accept that lack of access to scientific information leads to poorer health care and that sub-optimal health care costs lives?

Is it ethical to withhold information from those who need it most?

In a survey conducted by MalariaWorld, a scientific and social online network for professionals in the field, more than three-quarters of researchers based in the developing world not only considered limited access to be unethical, but also felt that it could potentially cost lives. But the world is finally waking up. Elsevier, one of the world's leading academic publishers, has received a painful blow since the launch of the global petition thecostofknowledge.com, which encourages scientists to stop submitting manuscripts to Elsevier, stop reviewing manuscripts submitted to their journals and discontinue any editorial work with the publisher. As of July

2012, more than 12,000 scientists around the world had signed the petition. This 'academic spring' was fuelled by prohibitive journal subscription rates, Elsevier's lobbying against open access and the cost of accessing material behind the paywall (downloading a single article costs on average US$30). When Harvard University's Winston Hide published his resignation as associate editor of Elsevier's journal *Genomics* in the *Guardian* in May 2012, it became international news. 'No longer can I work for a system that provides solid profits for the publisher while effectively denying colleagues in developing countries access to research findings,' he wrote. The day I read Hide's letter I handed in my resignation as editorial board member for Elsevier's journal *Acta Tropica*.

The open access movement has grown massively. But often with this model, the source of the profit comes from the authors themselves, who pay to have their work published. Once again we are faced with a situation where those in the northern hemisphere can cover publication costs relatively easily, yet developing country scientists are stuck because they cannot afford to pay to publish in open access journals (this cost frequently exceeds US$1,200 per submission). When they do decide to pay, they must use funds that would have otherwise gone towards further research. More than 60 per cent of respondents to the MalariaWorld survey based in developing countries considered open access publication costs to be 'high' or 'too high'. When they are unable to cover these costs, researchers are destined to return to closed access publishers with the knowledge that their peers may never see their work.

When living in Zambia, Tanzania, and Kenya over a period of 11 years, my wife and I witnessed first hand how the lack of access to scientific information about malaria hinders progress. It inspired us to set up MalariaWorld. What started out as a small-scale effort grew into a free service now reaching more than 7,500 professionals in more than 140 countries. MalariaWorld provides daily updates of newly-released scientific articles, publishes editorials and expert opinions, hosts discussion forums, stimulates debate and encourages networking so research can be practically applied. In 2010, we launched a true open access journal, the *MalariaWorld Journal*, where academics don't pay to publish and don't pay to read. We call this 'open access 2.0'. We cover the costs of editorial work and online publishing simply by tapping financial resources from parties other than authors or readers. A grant from the Netherlands Organisation for Scientific Research has enabled us to cover the cost of publishing the next 90 articles.

When it comes to malaria, both restricted and open access publishing have serious negative implications for those working in developing countries, creating disparity and inequitable distribution of knowledge. This negatively affects the quality of healthcare, which is likely to cost lives. It's not surprising, therefore, that across the developing world, more than 95 per cent of our survey respondents agreed or strongly agreed to the statement: 'Scientific articles on malaria should be available for free to all in need of it'. It is high time that academic publishers rethink the ramifications of their business model. ☐

©Bart GJ Knols
41(3): 115/120
DOI: 10.1177/0306422012456482
www.indexoncensorship.org

Bart GJ Knols is a malariologist, entrepreneur and author. He has a PhD in medical entomology and is the founder of MalariaWorld

OPEN KNOWLEDGE

US legislation may force all journals to make publicly funded work freely available. **Doug Rocks-Macqueen** asks why the proposal has not been universally welcomed

In the May/June issue of *Archaeology* magazine the president of the Archaeological Institute of America (AIA), Elizabeth Bartman, made a statement that resulted in an out-cry from archaeologists: 'We at the Archaeological Institute of America (AIA), along with our colleagues at the American Anthropological Association and other learned societies, have taken a stand against open access.'

The story of Bartman's opposi-tion to the public dissemination of knowledge broke in mid-April and by the end of the month she had made a partial retraction on the AIA's website following strong nega-tive attention in the press.

In her retraction, Bartman stated that she was 'not against open access as a concept' but was 'opposed to slated government legis-lation on the issue'. This was a direct reference to the Federal Research Public Access Act, currently working its way through US Congress. The bill would require that the results of any project funded by the US govern-ment be made open access after a fixed period of time.

In her statement against open access, Bartman quoted parts of the institute's mission: 'Believing that greater understanding of the past enhances our shared sense of humanity and enriches our exis-tence, the AIA seeks to educate people of all ages about the signifi-cance of archaeological discovery.'

So why would the AIA come out against a proposal that meets its mission statement? The institute puts it down to costs:

We fear that this legislation would prove damaging to the traditional venues in which scientific informa-tion is presented by offer-ing, for no cost, something that has considerable costs associated with producing it. It would undermine, and ultimately dismantle, by of-fering for no charge, what subscribers actually support financially – a rigorous pub-lication process that does serve the public, because it results in superior work.

Publishing can certainly be expensive and it is not always possible to rely on donations or the taxpayer to pick up the bill. The fear of publishers and societies is that if they give away their journals for free then no one will pay to be a member. Taking this fear into consideration, the stance of the AIA against open access is logical: they are scared of losing their members and being forced to close down.

However, when looking at the facts, this sympathetic reasoning starts to fall apart. The National Science Foundation, providing almost the only US government funds used for projects that appear in archaeology journals, supports roughly 50 archaeology projects a year. At best, no more than 55 projects in any given year would have to be made open access if the Federal Research Public Access Act were to be made law. The AIA only publishes one periodical publication, the *American Journal of Archaeology* (AJA). There are over 250 English language periodical publications that specialise in archaeology. If one were to include journals in related subjects such as anthropology, history or classics, this number jumps into the thousands. Include cross-disciplinary publications, and the possible locations for one to publish research jump to tens of thousands of options. Fifty-five publications spread out over hundreds, thousands or possibly tens of thousands of journals – and one might speculate that, at most, every year the AIA would have to make one or two of their articles open access.

The institute's reference to the 'considerable costs' involved in publishing is a questionable assertion. As pointed out by many open access advocates, the cost of starting and running a journal is quite low – some put the number at as little as $350 annually for a bare-bones operation relying on volunteers. This type of operation is not too different from how the AJA is currently run. All of the writing of the articles and research is done for free. The peer review process, which according to the AIA provides benefit to the public, is all done by volunteers. There is no reason why that should not continue. The AIA could even move to a print-on-demand system where those who want print copies can pay for them. This would significantly cut costs while allowing everyone to access the information.

Looking at the facts, it would seem that the AIA may have overreacted. But, to return to my original question: why would the institute overreact to something that is likely to help them fulfil their mission 'to educate people of all ages about the significance of archaeological discovery'? Why would the AIA, or any other scholarly or disciplinary society, come

NAME	REVENUE	BUDGET SPENT ON PUBLISHING	MONEY BROUGHT IN BY PUBLISHING	TOP EMPLOYEE PAY	SOURCE
American Chemical Society (2010)	$508,206,902	$340,437,402 (information services)	$421,489,737 (information services)	$1,084,417	portal.acs.org
American Society for Nutrition (2008)	$10,785,223	$2,663,197 (only 2 journals)	$3,762,943 (only 2 journals)	$330,478	www.eri-nonprofit-salaries.com
Phycological Society of America (2010)	$153,426,705	$34,274,251	$80,765,686	$618.883	www.apa.org
American Institute of Physics (2010)	$74,434,904	$53,845,932	$58,717,826	$461,744	www.eri-nonprofit-salaries.com
Institute of Electrical and Electronics Engineers (2010)	$850,608,457	$117,931,932	$127,642,124	$728,442	www.ieee.org/about
American Society of Hematology (2009)	$97,694,579	$7,828,861	$ 9,668,725	$535,933	www.eri-nonprofit-salaries.com
Archaeological Institute of America (2010)	$6,725,435	$4,153,916	$4,677,349	$134,323	www.archaeological.org
Protein Society	$1,474,097	$51,942	$189,339	$200,887	www.eri-nonprofit-salaries.com
American Institute of Aeronautics and Astronautics (2011)	$23,215,000	$4,388,000	$5,938,000		www.aiaa.org
American Sociological Association (2010)	$6,891,243	$1,004,735	$2,674,776	$240,558	www.eri-nonprofit-salaries.com
Seismological Society of America (2010)	$ 1,664,414	$995,292	$1,365,258	$122,294	www.eri-nonprofit-salaries.com
Ecological Society of America (2009)	$6,807,123	$2,607,173	$3,179,763	$238,943	www.eri-nonprofit-salaries.com
The American Society of Plant Biologists (2010)	$6,892,578	$3,083,531	$5,134,845	$200,810	www.eri-nonprofit-salaries.com
American Association for Dental Research (2010)	$2,214,921	$145,447	$238,615	$213,526	www.eri-nonprofit-salaries.com

out against the idea that the public should have access to the research they paid for?

One possible explanation is that many scholarly societies, for all their rhetoric and not-for-profit status, are actually knowledge cartels – controlling the supply of information in their field and profiting from restricting access. They have neglected their original scholarly purpose of disseminating knowledge to all and now dedicate a significant proportion of their resources to publishing which also makes up the vast majority of its costs and 'profits'. Its 990 tax form shows that in 2011 it spent $350,281 on its journal and $373,818 on its societies and national lecture programme. In addition to the journal, the AIA also publishes a magazine, which is available on newsstands. It was responsible for $3,803,635 of costs and $4,299,630 of revenue.

There is also great incentive for the people who manage and run these organisations to defend their cartel. For example, the American Chemical Society, a huge opponent of open access, pays many of its employees, as reported in their 990 tax return, over six figures. These salaries range from $304,528 to $1,084,417 in 2010.

Beyond salaries, these organisations provide other benefits to their employees. According to its tax return, the Phycological Society of America provided one of its employees with a mortgage worth $300,000 at an interest rate of 3.15 per cent in 2004. Even with the current record low rates, most people could not obtain such a favourable deal. While these societies are not-for-profits, their employees are heavily financially invested in their organisations bringing in the revenue to support six-figure salaries and perks.

Most of the societies that opposed or were critical of open access in the White House's consultation receive a good portion of their funding from publishing; for some it's over 80 per cent of their revenue. Some of these societies are in essence publishers with an individual subscription option attached to their publications, called a membership.

Open access is a direct attack on the business models of these societies. While mandated open access may not directly hurt societies, by forcing them to make some of their articles freely available it will become a competitor and one that they will be hard pressed to beat. It will have all the benefits of their own publications, peer review, volunteer work, but people will be able to access it for free.

Whether it is right or wrong for scholarly societies to operate as knowledge cartels may be a matter of moral opinion. Some might say that they are not following their mission statements and should be stripped of their not-for-profit/charity status. Others would argue that while they may not benefit society as a whole, they do provide a service to their members. What is clear is that there is a vested interest in controlling the flow of information. ❑

41(3): 122/126
DOI: 10.1177/0306422012457748
www.indexoncensorship.org

Doug Rocks-Macqueen is a graduate student in archaeology at the University of Edinburgh

FALSE FREEDOMS

Before the 2003 invasion, free speech was constantly under threat. But, says **May Witwit**, universities today remain gripped by fear

It is hard to appreciate freedom until you experience losing it. It may be difficult for someone born in a democracy to understand, but it's somewhat like comparing what a wild bird feels when locked in a cage, as opposed to a bird born in captivity that regards a cage as its natural environment. When I am asked about academic freedom in Iraq, it is this parallel that leaps to mind. As a former lecturer at the University of Baghdad who has recently completed a PhD in the UK, I have felt the difference acutely.

Elder members of my family have always commented that we Iraqis are as extreme as our weather, which is bitterly cold in the winter and burning hot in summer. In a country like Iraq, where all aspects of life are interrelated, there are no clear boundaries separating the social and the personal from the professional. Friendships, personal contacts and family relationships are greatly influential when it comes to careers and professional and academic progress. Differences in opinion or criticism of a particular topic of research or a professional practice (even if objective) can be easily misinterpreted as personal criticism and may result in long-term animosity. In most cases it is either black or white, and colleagues in academia, like colleagues in other sectors, are either friends to be supported and encouraged or enemies to be fought or removed. Although some Iraqis may not agree, I speak from my experience and question the existence of real freedom, whether academic or otherwise.

Unfortunately, the term freedom, more often than not, is mistakenly associated with the Arabic concept of immorality. This misinterpretation, in my view, is a major obstacle, hindering the development of the very concept of freedom in Iraq. When freedom becomes a risk, threatening every aspect of human survival, people resort to performance, putting on a show to prove that they are doing what's expected of them, forgetting what they really want or believe in. They practise a form of self-censorship to protect themselves.

Thinking back to 2000, when I had to choose a topic for my MA dissertation at the University of Baghdad, I see a clear example of how individual academics can become accomplices in not only the mechanisms of state censorship, but also in social and religious censorship. Fascinated by Tennyson's encapsulation of the past and the present in his *Idylls of the King*, I wanted to explore the concept of sin through the image of Guinevere across the ages, beginning with Sir Thomas Malory's *Le Morte d'Arthur* in the 15th century.

Before attempting to write the outline for my dissertation, I consulted one of my professors, a distinguished female scholar whose excellent knowledge of the Victorian age had triggered my interest in that era. She advised me against the project and warned me that it would be regarded as outrageous, obscene and might even get me into trouble. Though very disappointed, I knew she was right and if I were to insist it would be regarded as a breach of our culture's assumed moral code. Sin is a taboo subject and, as a respectable married woman, the concept should 'never cross my mind'. I turned my thoughts to Samuel Beckett and modern drama but the problem this time was different: if I were to choose this topic, my supervisor would be a man. It would be difficult to contact him at all times or discuss issues freely and it might even trigger social disapproval because my husband was working abroad. I preferred to avoid creating these sorts of problems for myself. I was not interested in literary criticism or in the Restoration poets like Pope and Dryden, but the professor who lectured us on the Restoration period was German and I sought her advice because I felt she would be more open-minded towards sensitive topics and might even suggest more interesting ideas than the ones I had in mind. The professor was interested in Chaucer, whom I had never heard of before, as his work was taught only to PhD-level students. She suggested I read *The Canterbury Tales* and also Dickens's *Our Mutual Friend* and other books during the summer holidays and to choose a topic for my research before her return to Baghdad in September. *The Canterbury Tales* captured my interest and soon the idea of researching the theme of love in the *Tales* took hold. The professor did not object and I submitted my outline for research on 'The Theme of Love in Chaucer's *Canterbury Tales*'. I avoided going into details about physical love in *The Canterbury Tales* and focused on the less problematic types of love, such as gluttony, parental love, divine love and the love of worldly things.

At that time in Iraq, just before the invasion in 2003, the use of the internet was limited to a few privileged people and important offices and departments in the various ministries. Under the UN-imposed sanctions on Iraq, the most recent books available in our libraries were publications Iraq had looted from Kuwaiti libraries during Iraq's 1990 invasion, but I needed updated material. A former colleague and friend who worked at the internet department in one of the ministries offered to help. I could not believe my luck, but I soon saw how useless this resource was. Every time I typed the word 'love' into the search engine I was denied access, and so I had to make do with the texts and the books from Kuwait.

The US-led invasion of Iraq did not open doors or offer freedom to Iraqis; instead, it created chaos. The political, social and religious subjugation of the individual remained the same. US soldiers represented the new authority and soon they began to demonstrate their superiority and control. Many people lost their lives because some soldier felt like it. Atrocities silenced Iraqis; there was a climate of fear. Soldiers broke many taboos. For example, during their searches and raids, they entered women's bedrooms; often women were either still in bed or in their nightwear. Since Arab and Muslim traditions do not permit strangers to see women's bedrooms or see women in nightwear, this was a real problem. Many of my female students complained that they woke up to find soldiers tampering with the contents of their wardrobes and drawers. This angered the male members of the family very much, but fear of being shot or detained in one of the many military camps on suspicion of terrorism silenced them. Signs reading 'Deadly force. Keep 100 meters away' on US military vehicles also frightened people, including myself, because it clearly reflected that these soldiers were authorised to kill. People's silence encouraged further breaches from the US forces that sometimes led to the confiscation of cash and women's jewellery (an Iraqi woman's mobile bank account) during raids.

The restrictions governing academic freedom and freedom of expression remained more or less the same before and after the 2003 invasion. The brief freedom witnessed during the transitional period under the US-led Coalition Provisional Authority (CPA) and the Iraqi Governing Council was marked by

chaos, not least because people had no genuine understanding of how democracy works. Academic institutions were no exception. I still remember how, on our first day back at university after the US-led invasion of Iraq, my students turned their backs to the blackboard and faced the window. Unable to understand their behaviour, I asked why. To my surprise, they happily answered: 'It is the age of democracy and we are free to do as we like.' Similar actions occurred in other places, such as petrol stations, where drivers broke the long queue and hailed the new democracy and freedom. During that time, many academics were not as interested in research as they were busy trying to adjust to new problems, such as shortages in electricity, fuel, food and other necessities.

Because of fear, Iraqis' supposed new-found freedom of expression was limited to criticism of these new problems, non-sensitive issues that had not existed during the former regime: lack of water, electricity, health services and corruption in general. Academics were also affected. As intellectuals and leaders in their society, they probably had a deeper understanding of the consequences of voicing criticism about effects of the invasion. The cries for a better standard of living and better services went unheard, reminding me of how Iraqis currently describe the different stages they have been through: they say that the former regime sellotaped mouths, the Americans removed the sellotape and the present regime wears earplugs. This, of course, does not quite reflect the truth, as the current regime is also guilty of censorship and of silencing critical voices.

When the 2005 elections gave prominence to the Islamic parties, Iraqis were back to square one. This time more complicated religious and conventional restrictions dominated life, including academia. Ordinary citizens and intellectuals alike advocated new ideas, many of which contradicted the ones they previously held, in order to conform to the new prevailing ideology of the influential political 'Islamic' parties. Religious rituals began to take place inside universities, and walls were covered with posters of prominent clerics and other influential individuals, advising women to wear the hijab. Previous conformists were called insurgents and were outlawed; highly qualified professors were dismissed on the pretext of Ba'ath Party membership. Many academics left the country and those unable to do so complied and obeyed, out of opportunism or fear. Within a short period of time the number of women who wore the hijab, including academics, outnumbered uncovered women; prominent male scholars grew beards and wore rings as a sign of their loyalty to a certain faith – evidence that Iraqis continued to lack not only academic freedom but also all kinds of social, intellectual and religious freedoms necessary for independent thinking. The conversion of

Baghdad University, 26 October 2008
Credit: Hadi Mizban/AP

many academics from one faction to another suggests a survival tactic to achieve personal goals and to maintain professional and social positions.

I left Iraq in late 2008, when it became impossible to continue as an independent-thinking secular female university lecturer. The sheer refusal to conform posed a serious threat to my safety. Although I am no longer part of the academic milieu in Iraq, I continue to follow the developments there through contacts or by reading whatever literature or research papers I can get my hands on. In formal university or ministry of higher education policies and regulations, there is no mention of restrictions on academic research or teaching. Yet an academic or teacher should consider the consequences before attempting to tackle a 'daring' topic. Lecturers of English literature in many Iraqi universities, for example, now avoid the mention of physical or sensual topics in English and American novels to avoid being accused of corrupting young minds. Recently, the Minister of Higher Education attempted to strip a female academic from the University of Baghdad of her doctorate in Political Sciences because of a questionnaire she published as part of her dissertation: its results revealed that the al Maliki government was regarded by participants as the worst in Iraq's history. The minister demanded that the content of the academic's thesis be changed to favour al Maliki. Although the doctorate was finally approved following an appeal to the University Council, I doubt that many others would be tempted to follow in this academic's footsteps.

A recent study on female academics in Iraq found that they do not have equal access to training, conference participation or research, though the study did not expand on points affecting academics as compared with the general female population in the country. My next project will examine the decline in the position of women since 2005, looking specifically at the increase of al Muta'a in Iraq. The practice, in which women are exploited under the pretext of a short-term marriage that may last for hours, days or months, has been increasingly encouraged and given legitimacy over the last few years. No longer an academic in Iraq, I feel able to take on this subject. But currently, in Iraq, it would be impossible to carry out research on this topic. ❏

©May Witwit
41(3): 127/132
DOI: 10.1177/0306422012456140
www.indexoncensorship.org

May Witwit is an honorary research fellow at the University of Bedfordshire

MEMORY LOSS

The Second World War has cult status in Belarus where its history is beyond questioning. **David R Marples** has first-hand experience of the heavy hand of the state

For the past three years I have been working on the topic of memory and war in Belarus. Like any visitor to that country– and I have been going there for the past 20 years regularly – I was fascinated and intrigued by the prevalence of Second World War memorials. No matter where one went, there was a war monument. The most important official occasions in the country, especially Independence Day on 3 July, are commemorations of the war. At those times, the capital Minsk hosts an elaborate military parade attended by President Alexander Lukashenko and his third son Mikalay, who was born in 2004. Both, improbably, wear the uniform of a general.

There are a growing number of historic sites of significance in Belarus. Some date from Soviet times, such as the Khatyn Memorial Complex and the Brest Hero Fortress. Others are of more recent origin, such as the Stalin Line Museum near Zaslavl, some 27km from Minsk. Monuments abound, mostly but not always in memory of partisan heroes, such as 14-year-old Marat Kazey, who died after an encounter with the German occupants, or Konstantin Zaslonov, also known as partisan leader Dyadya Kostya, who died in the village of Kupovat, Vitsebsk region, on

14 November 1942, and now has a statue in his memory at the railway station in Vorsha.

The focus on the war is hardly surprising. Belarus lost, according to official figures, about one-third of its population during the war years. It suffered a brutal occupation. Its Jewish population was virtually wiped out. Many villages and settlements were destroyed. The city of Minsk lost its entire centre.

Still, it seemed to me that the war, which ended 67 years ago, was also an instrument of nation-building. Lukashenko became president in July 1994, and has remained in place by cowing his opponents and manipulating elections, as well as by maintaining a largely state-run economy sponsored by cheap Russian imports for many years. Like many dictators or would-be dictators, one facet of his leadership has been a constant quest for legitimacy. He has found it in part by identifying his regime with the wartime Soviet republic, and by raising the war to the status of a modern-day cult, the events of which can no longer be questioned.

My study was not the usual historian's route of heading for the National Archives and requesting permission to examine various documents, though I have done that in the past. I was more concerned with the dissemination and narratives of the war permeating through the media, school textbooks, historic sites and monuments. Most interesting of all was the question of generations: how could genuine links be formed between the remaining war veterans, who are now over 85 years of age, and schoolchildren?

I found Belarusians ready to assist at every point. Friends, acquaintances, librarians, politicians, newspaper editors and journalists all came to my aid. I visited all the sites named above, some of them more than once. I spent hours in the Museum of the Great Patriotic War in Minsk. I perused newspapers from different regions of the country to read their accounts of the war. I grabbed every school textbook on which I could lay hands, purchasing many of them in local bookstores. I watched TV documentaries, the recent Russian-Belarusian film about the Brest Fortress, visited exhibits at the Minsk Museum of History and wandered through a number of villages and towns to locate monuments. Now at the stage of writing up some conclusions, I am even more convinced that the usage of the war is largely, though not totally, state propaganda.

One point needs to be stressed at the outset. Though about one-third of Belarus's war victims were Jews, the Holocaust is not a major topic. It is barely mentioned in school textbooks. Most of the monuments and sites do not distinguish between Jewish and general Soviet deaths, following the practices of the old USSR. Monuments to the Holocaust are usually funded from abroad. The contemporary glorification of the war is about partisans rather than Jews, though sometimes the two were synonymous, as anyone who has watched the 2008 film *Defiance*, starring Daniel Craig, will testify.

Another controversial issue is anti-Soviet opposition during the war. Officially approved texts contain a statement that they have the approval of the Ministry of Education. One will search in vain for any information about how the population of Belarus first received news about the war, even though many initially welcomed the invaders. Rather, one hears about the treachery of the attack, the brave response and defensive battles to slow down the attackers, and the unity of the population against the enemy. Little distinction is made between the former term 'Soviet' to describe inhabitants and the current 'Belarusian'. It is as though the population of the republic were fighting for an independent state.

Admittedly this is not an ethnic entity. All sources note that various people contributed to the defense of Belarus, including Tatars, Kazakhs, and of course Russians. At the same time the Belarusian component receives emphasis, as do those ethnic Belarusians who received the coveted title of Hero of the Soviet Union.

The year 1941 was once billed as a year to be forgotten for the USSR, which appeared unprepared for the timing and scale of the invasion and lost vast territories and most of its industry to the invaders. It has now been resurrected and transformed into a time of defiant resistance. The narrative begins with the defense of the Brest Fortress, where a small group held out for a few weeks before surrendering to the Germans. It continues with the Stalin Line, which, one historian told me, delayed the Germans in their march to Moscow to the extent that Stalin was able to summon forces from the Far East and save Moscow. Succinctly put: the Belarusians saved the Soviet capital.

Among others, the German historian Christian Ganzer has largely demythologised the Brest Fortress story. The Germans had occupied Smolensk by the time it was captured. The Stalin Line is completely mythical. It had been demolished before the Germans even got there as the Soviet border moved westward after the Nazi-Soviet Pact. Historians discovered some years ago that even the destruction of the village of Khatyn, site of an infamous massacre, was undertaken by auxiliary police, allegedly as retribution for the death on this same day of German Olympic gold medalist Hans Woellke near Khatyn, at the hands of Soviet partisans.

The partisans are a different matter. Belarus was certainly the centre of the partisan movement, but there is no consensus on when and how

Second World War memorial in the former village of Khatyn, northeast of Minsk, 7 May 2011
Credit: Vasily Fedosenko/Reuters

it began. Ultimately it was subordinated to the NKVD, and the Belarusian party leadership under Panteleimon Ponomarenko, one of Stalin's cruellest and most devoted henchmen. If one adds up figures from official accounts of partisan destruction, one learns that they destroyed 28 trains and killed 1,500 Germans *daily* in 1943–4. No further comment is needed.

By the summer of 1943, the partisans had grown into a mass movement. The following year they coalesced into the Red Army, which destroyed the German Army Group Centre in Operation Bagration. Without doubt they played an important role. But how were they regarded by the local population, which had to feed and billet them?

In 2010, local historian Illya Kopyl published a lengthy and critical series about the partisans in the opposition newspaper *Narodnaya Volya*, focusing on their exploitation of local residents. The result was a picketing of the offices of the newspaper by veterans (some of whom appeared to be too young to have served in the war) and members of the Belarusian Union of Patriotic Youth, an organisation loyal to the president. The newspaper received a warning from the Ministry of Information for 'Disseminating false information that discredits the guerilla movement in Belarus, [and] actions of the Red Army during the Great Patriotic War'. Kopyl was guilty of 'historical revisionism'.

I studied this term at some length because it appears often. Belarusian officials, particularly from the Ministry of Defence, will make comments to the effect that the memory of the war must never be forgotten, but some people would like to change the facts and rewrite its history. They are historical revisionists who should be condemned because the history of the war is sacred and cannot be altered.

This sort of rhetoric sounds laughable but it has serious consequences. It means first of all that it is very difficult for Belarusian historians to attempt serious studies of many facets of the war. To do so means risking their careers and incomes, and being designated as hostile to the prevailing line, ie the view perpetuated by the Lukashenko regime, which can be described as the Soviet line with a Belarusian angle.

In challenging the official view of the war, historians are potentially undermining the entire history curriculum in schools, which regards the war as the defining event in the Belarusian past, to the virtual exclusion of all others. In most areas of life, the Republic of Belarus is a very different place from Soviet Belarus, but not in the field of 20th-century history. Opponents of the Soviets were bourgeois nationalists, collaborators with the enemy, people who sought to undermine Soviet power, just as the modern opposition in Belarus is often dismissed by the phrase 'enemies of the people' or a 'fifth column' (most recently linked to Germans and Poles).

Revisionists are also challenging a linkage between the Belarusian state of 1945 and the modern version. One Belarusian historian has noted that the word 'repressions' has been removed from textbooks. In the same way, the crimes during Stalinism have also been largely concealed. After the war, many Belarusian partisan leaders were treated with suspicion. The Minsk underground was suspected of treachery. On the orders of Ponomarenko, hundreds of underground defenders of Minsk were arrested after the war and spent up to 15 years in labour camps. Not until after the death of Stalin were Belarusian 'achievements' in the war recognised. Minsk did not receive its current status of 'hero city' until 1974, 30 years after its liberation from the occupants.

But the Lukashenko regime refuses to focus on Stalinist crimes, such as the executions at Kurapaty (1937-41), where the NKVD executed up to

250,000 people. It denied until recently that the Katyn massacres of Polish officers in Russia included any Polish prisoners from Belarus. Yet recent research by Natalia Lebedeva has confirmed that 1,996 Poles from Western Belarus were among the NKVD victims executed at camps in Kozelsk and Ostashkov (Russia), and Starobelsk (Ukraine).

Lukashenko himself has always seemed ambivalent about Stalin, and reluctant to divulge the extent of the purges in Belarus. The bust of Stalin at the entrance to the Stalin Line Museum is usually adorned with wreaths. The logical deduction is that exposure of the enormity of Stalinist crimes may undermine the myths of the Great Patriotic War in which so many loyal Stalinists served. The regime itself continues to enhance the power and scope of the operations of the KGB. Belarus is thus maintaining the Stalinist legacy.

This summer I had hoped to make a concluding visit to Belarus for the purposes of this study. But my visa application to the Belarusian Embassy in Ottawa was refused. I never did find out why, despite several requests for an explanation. Either it was something to do with the nature of this study, or else my name was added to a 'blacklist' of those to be refused entry, along with the list of undesirables (mostly opposition members) prevented from leaving the country.

In several respects the 'Partisan Republic' is still fighting enemies, real and mythical, in a world that seems detached from reality. Like Stalin, Lukashenko imagines himself surrounded by enemies and hostile forces. By controlling the publicity and interpretations of the Great Patriotic War, the regime hopes to create its own legacy as a destroyer of fascism, while denying much of the Belarusian past, culture, and continuing the Soviet neglect of the native language. It is a slippery slope, and will be even more precarious once, as is inevitable, the veterans pass on and there is no one to take part in the ritual of parades and commemorations. ❒

©David R Marples
41(3): 133/138
DOI: 10.1177/0306422012457126
www.indexoncensorship.org

David R Marples is distinguished university professor, Department of History and Classics, University of Alberta, Canada. He is author of 14 books and the president of the North American Association for Belarusian Studies

LAST WORD

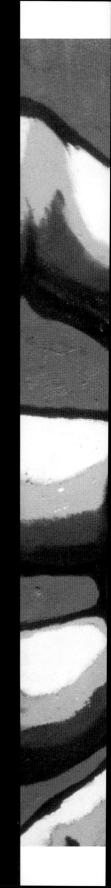

Mural commemorating the disappeared, Buenos Aires, Argentina
Credit: Christophe Bluntzer/Imagestate Media Partners Limited – Impact Photos/Alamy

ART OF RESISTANCE

A new exhibition showcases Syrian artists pioneering new channels for defiance. Co-curator **Malu Halasa** salutes an explosion of creative dissent

Every revolution produces its own imagery. The collective Alshaab Alsori Aref Tarekh ('the Syrian people know their way') challenges nearly 50 years of monolithic Ba'ath Party iconography in their political posters, currently on show in the exhibition *Culture in Defiance: Continuing Traditions of Satire, Art and the Struggle for Freedom in Syria*. The significance of these new posters, available as print on demand online, was put into perspective for me by the exhibition's fellow curator Aram Tahhan, who once stayed in a military-owned hotel. 'Everywhere there were pictures of Bashar al Assad or his father, his three children, his martyr brother and sometimes his elegant wife. These prevented the residents from appearing in the corridors in their swimming suits, presumably to protect the modesty of the president.' Sometimes the messages of a brutal state can live in unexpected ways in the minds of the subjugated.

My love affair with Syria began long before I co-curated *Culture in Defiance*. I saw Damascus for the first time when I was 16. In my early 20s, as a young journalist, I lived there one summer with Palestinian *fedayeen* as I moved in and out of war-torn Beirut writing my first big feature.

From 2000 onwards, I regularly returned for work and pleasure, which included researching the book *The Secret Life of Syrian Lingerie* with Rana Salam. In the basements of the racy lingerie factories, conducting lengthy interviews with the religious men who designed and manufactured bras and panties that sang, lit up or fell apart at the sound of a hand clap, Rana and I came close to understanding what could only be described as a uniquely Syrian national character. It can blend manufacturing inventiveness with pragmatism, and spirituality with a wicked sense of humour. The men and the women we interviewed were forthright and generous.

So last year, when I started seeing the bombs beginning to fall in Syria on my television screen in London, it was like watching friends face down a military onslaught. No right-thinking individual, I thought to myself, could stand by, and say and do nothing.

The idea for the exhibition grew after a number of meetings and events with Syrians in London. I had been running after the Syrian cartoonist Ali Ferzat for a lengthy *Index* interview and his words were ringing in my ears: 'I haven't seen the British, Dutch or French demonstrating against what's happening in Syria in the way they demonstrated against the Vietnam war.' After the launch of his exhibition in London in March, the Syrian journalist and translator Leen Zyiad, Reel Syria's Dan Gorman, his wife Yasmin and I, shared a taxi while rushing to catch a lecture by the Italian visual critic Donatella Della Ratta. On the way, we discussed how the violence in Syria had effectively obscured the country's new art of resistance, and exchanged ideas on the best way of bringing this work to a wider audience in the West.

Donatella's illustrated talk included remarkable user-generated internet footage by Syrian artists, animators and activists – all of it produced since the revolution began – and made it apparent that an exhibition was urgently needed. Eventually Donatella joined Leen, Aram and I in curating *Culture in Defiance*, with the support of the Prince Claus Fund. Alongside the cartoons of Ali Ferzat, the exhibition features the first series of the cyber-puppet play *Top Goon: Diaries of a Little Dictator*.

Through the use of finger puppets, which are easy to smuggle through checkpoints, the anonymous Syrian artists' group Masasit Mati captures not only the insecurity of a regime but also the nuanced nature of Syrian politics. In one episode, Hafez al Assad appears as a long murderous shadow over the entire country. But puppet semantics are not one-sided, as explained by director Jameel – who always appears masked in public. 'The purpose of our art is to address Syria – all of the country, the Syria that's revolting, the silent Syria and the regime as well,' he told me.

At the heart of the exhibition is the mass creative dissent that has been taking place in Syrian cities through song, dance and illustration. In the publication that accompanies the exhibition are cartoons from Amude, a largely Kurdish town on the border of Turkey, and birthplace of Abdulbaset Sieda, who was appointed, in June, as the new president of the main opposition group, the Syrian National Council. Drawing satirical cartoons does not come easily to people who have never lampooned their political leaders because of draconian defamation laws, which could land them in jail, facing torture and a five-year sentence.

Like most of the anonymous work featured in the Prince Claus Fund gallery, our two Syrian curators – Leen and Aram – understandably use pseudonyms. There are exceptions: contributors to veteran Syrian artist Youssef Abdelki's Facebook page Art.Liberte.Syria, better known as Art and Freedom, sign their work in solidarity with the thousands of victims and prisoners of the uprising. Another engaged artist, Khalil Younes, has been inspired by Goya and produces powerful pen and ink drawings of Syrian martyrs that have gone viral over the internet or have been turned into stencils on Syrian streets.

It was nearly impossible for us to find high resolution imagery of the graffiti that started the revolution, since both spray painting and documenting it are highly dangerous pursuits. Don Karl, from Here to Fame Publishing in Berlin, came up with a timely solution. He sent his co-editor of *Arabic Graffiti*, Arabic type designer and typographer Pascal Zoghbi, onto the streets of Beirut. His pictures captured the remnants of Freedom Graffiti Week Syria, an international campaign in the spring that roused the ire of pro-Assad forces who vandalised the street art.

The voices of ordinary people close the exhibition. After being obscured and silenced by decades of dictatorship, the Syrians are finally telling the world who they really are. The dreams they have for their future are not so very different from our own. ❒

Malu Halasa
41(3): 141/152
DOI: 10.1177/0306422012456135
www.indexoncensorship.org

Malu Halasa is a writer and editor. Her books include *Transit Tehran* (Garnet Publishing). *Culture in Defiance: Continuing Traditions of Satire, Art and the Struggle for Freedom in Syria* at the Prince Claus Fund Gallery in Amsterdam is curated by Malu Halasa, Aram Tahhan, Leen Zyiad and Donatella Della Ratta and continues until 23 November.

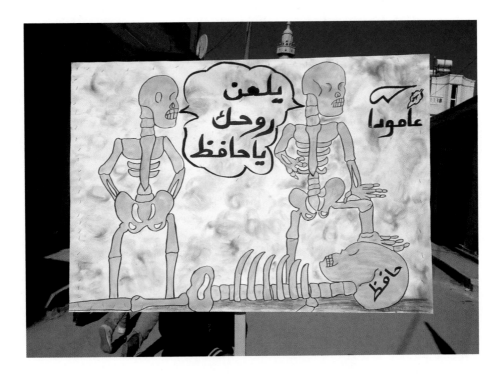

الدفاع عن النفس حق مشروع

الشعب السوري عارف طريقه

حريتي خارج جمالي لا

I dreamt of getting   married,
buying   an   ordinary   car,
          having a nice family,
working diligently
          and staying away from trouble.
I wanted to lead a simple
and   peaceful life,
          like any other young man.
Things have changed now   —
          I want to liberate my homeland,
restore   the   dignity   of
          my people and society
                    and
hold my head high and proudly say,
          "I am a Muslim Arab Syrian,
               in the land of the free."
The question is not whether
my   country
          is going to be liberated or not,
it is:
am I going to be alive to witness it
                    ?

Captions

Page 144: Beeshu, the president of Syria and starring finger puppet of Top Goon: Diaries of a Little Dictator. *Photograph courtesy of Masasit Mati, 2011*

Page 145: Both cartoons are from, and signed in the name of, the mainly Kurdish town of Amude, northeast Syria

Top image: The genie asks Bashar: 'What is your command?' He answers: 'Enough time to destroy our people.' The words 'international community' appear on the magic lantern

Bottom image: Two skeletons cry out: 'Curse your soul, Hafez!' A bony foot has been placed on his skull

Page 146: Civil Defense Is a Legitimate Right *by the Syrian poster collective Alshab Alsori Aref Tarekh, 2011*

Page 147: My Beauty Out of My Freedom *by Alshab Alsori Aref Tarekh, 2011*

Page 148: Hamza Bakkour *(pen and ink, 40–50cm) by Khalil Younes, 2011*

Page 149: About a Young Man Called Kashoosh *(pen and ink, 30–40cm) by Khalil Younes, 2011*

Page 150: Homs, the Mother of All Heroes

Text reads: 'The king of the jungle rides a tank', a play on the meaning of Assad, 'lion', in Arabic. The Bashar/Hitler stencil, originally designed by Egyptian street artist el Teneen, one of the first to stencil around Tahrir Square in Cairo in 2011, has appeared in Lebanon, Palestine and Egypt. Photograph by Pascal Zoghbi, 2012

Page 151: Syrian protester Jamal al Fatwa's last Facebook entry before he was arrested. His corpse was returned to his family after he died under torture

Culture is a basic need.

Prince Claus Fund *for*
Culture and Development

Based on the principle that culture is a basic need, the Prince Claus Fund's mission is to actively seek cultural collaborations founded on equality and trust, with partners of excellence, in spaces where resources and opportunities for cultural expression, creative production and research are limited and cultural heritage is threatened.

Prince Claus Fund
Herengracht 603
1017 CE Amsterdam
The Netherlands
+31.20.344.9160

info@princeclausfund.nl
www.princeclausfund.org
facebook.com/princeclausfund

Fonds

Prince Claus Fund *for*
Culture and Development

THE PAST IN HIDING

Argentina's former dictator says he regrets nothing. **Andrew Graham-Yooll** considers a chilling reckoning in new revelations from the dirty war

Nearly four decades after the military coup of March 1976, Argentina is still coming to terms with the past. The intellectual conviction that societies can assimilate trauma by burying it in history books is yet to be realised, but the publication of two revelatory accounts this year offered the possibility of putting the record straight. In nine remarkable interviews with the imprisoned former dictator Jorge Rafael Videla, who ruled Argentina from 1976 until 1981, journalist Ceferino Reato provided a chilling description of the military plan to murder thousands of opponents in his book *Final Disposal*.

The second book, by Norma Morandini, a former journalist and now senator in Argentina's congress, is both a personal and moral exploration and an investigation of Argentine society in an attempt to explain the process of recovery from a state of denial. Her two younger siblings were 'disappeared' in September 1977. Morandini's revealing account begins in a comfortable middle-class world in central Argentina, then moves through loss and exile. She watches her mother emerge from grief and then enters battle to seek her lost children. When she returns to Argentina she is guilt-ridden for surviving, rejected for jobs and discriminated against for having dead or 'disappeared'

Writer and vice-presidential candidate Norma Morandini, whose siblings disappeared in 1977
Credit: Reuters

members of her family. She finally re-invents herself as a campaigner for a new culture in her country.

Argentina's dictatorship held power between 1976 and 1983. Although this was the shortest dictatorship of any in the region, the rule of the junta of three armed forces chiefs was the bloodiest; the only one that had a systematic plan to detain its captives in secret camps and make them disappear. It was Argentina that gave the word *'desaparecidos'* to the language of repression. Political groups and human rights organisations set the figure of disappeared at 30,000. But this has been an estimate, not backed by the recovery of remains and identities.

Ceferino Reato's book is subtitled 'The confessions of Videla about the *desaparecidos'*. The conversations between the former dictator and the journalist recall the late Gitta Sereny's interviews with the imprisoned Nazi Albert Speer. The 86-year-old Argentinian criminal appeared at once generous with information and coldly brutal in his view of events. On more than one occasion in his replies, Videla said he was merely acting as a military officer in his country's service.

'Let's say there were seven or eight thousand people who had to die to win this war: we could not execute them. How could we execute so many people?' Videla told Reato.

'The phrase Final Solution was never used. The words Final Disposal were used frequently: those are two very military words that mean taking out of service something that is useless. When, for example, you speak of old clothing which is no longer used or worn out, it is marked Final Disposal. That has no further useful life.'

Norma Morandini's book, *From Guilt to Forgiveness (De la culpa al perdón*, in Spanish), is a painful and very personal essay written ten years ago, but published only a few days after Reato's book last April. When I met her for an interview this summer, she rejected Videla's figures: 'If accepted they must be seen as the tally of the executioner. We can't simply believe the killer and not the victims ... During the trials of 1985 the figures and statements of the victims were put in doubt. For example, in those long hard six months of the trials of the juntas, former captives said that prisoners were drugged, tied, and dropped into the sea. Nothing happened. It was more than ten years later when the executioner, naval officer Adolfo Scilingo, confessed to Judge Baltasar Garzón in Spain that the account of the bodies thrown from planes was true. Then it was believed. Human behaviour makes it reasonable to give credit to the killer but not the victim.'

Formerly national deputy and now senator for a leftist alliance, Morandini studied medicine and psychology in her native Córdoba province, then became a journalist. She fled Argentina after the abduction of her brother and sister in 1977, went to Brazil and found asylum in Portugal. She then worked for the magazine *Cambio 16* in Spain, which was just trying out the discourse and freedoms of a new age after the death of Francisco Franco.

'We are a country that has not had a state policy to deal with events in our recent past. Our education does not include the construction of a culture of human rights.' These two sentences in part define the aim of Morandini's book, to develop a 'democratic society above the intolerance of the past'.

The statements made by Videla go a long way to help explain the failings of a society that allowed and even cheered the murderous military dictatorship that began in 1976. At the time, I was working at the English-language *Buenos Aires Herald*. 'Yes, but the guerrillas started killing first,' was often the rejoinder we got from readers and even officials, when editorially critical of the uniformed rulers. The guerrillas were not 'first', they were the product of the failure of constitutional government, of a whole society that considered itself the most modern and intellectually advanced in South America. The armed forces, formed into the most powerful party in the country since the 1930s, had hampered, disrupted and overthrown elected governments at will. Wrecking an elected government should have been considered a crime. And, we argued from the pages of Argentina's smallest daily, 'the state cannot descend to the level of its enemies, because killing people is wrong, whoever does it'. We did not get very far with that argument. When I quietly admitted to people that I had been an informant for Amnesty International since 1971 and writing for *Index on Censorship* since 1973, the ensuing question was: 'Yes, but what side are you on?' You had to take sides in the politics of a country that was descending into horror.

'To avoid arousing protests in or outside the country, we reached the decision that those people had to disappear; each disappearance can be understood as a certain masking, a disguise of a death', Videla told Ceferino Reato.

This blood-chilling comment takes me back to September 1976 and to a meeting at Government House in Buenos Aires attended by the then editor of the *Buenos Aires Herald*, Robert Cox, and myself as his news editor, with Videla's Secretary for Information, a naval captain named Carlos Carpintero. When we chided the minister about the secrecy and horror of the disappearances his rejoinder was: 'Do you want us to have all the adverse publicity that Chile has? No way. What would the IMF and all those international organisations say?' The flippant remark added to the horror. Robert Cox thought then that Videla was a dove among hawks. Since Reato's book appeared this spring, Cox has published two columns in the *Herald* stating that Hitler was alive and well and living in Argentina in the person of Jorge Rafael Videla. '[His] account of the holocaust unleashed on Argentina is notable for his lack of human decency and the cold-blooded manner in which he tells his story … I see a tactic behind Videla's confession. He has nothing to lose now, but by admitting responsibility for all the crimes committed while he was army commander and later de facto president, he has put a spanner in the works for trial judges who have to include him among all the accused who are currently on trial.'

The former dictator admitted to Reato that there were 'mistakes and excesses' but that was not the case 'with the disappeared', whose fate was part of a policy. The 'responsibility in each case fell to the regional commander,

who used the method he thought most appropriate. Each commander had full autonomy to find the quickest and least risky method. Nobody was against that ... I was not consulted. I consented by omission'. Elsewhere in the interview Videla said: 'Each commander was master and ruler over the life and death of each detainee.' And the method for disposing of bodies, that sinister 'Final Disposal', was equally the responsibility of unit commanders, no questions were asked among senior officers. They could bury the dead in mass graves, burn them in a stack of tyres, destroy them with lime.

The military handed over 227 children of captives to neighbours or relatives or to juvenile courts. Videla denies that there was 'an order to abduct minors. There were cases, I know, but they were the result of our lack of controls, there was no systematic plan to steal babies' from captured mothers. In spite of his denial, on 4 July a court sentenced Videla to 50 years in prison for planning and executing a systematic plan to remove and hide babies born in captivity. The Grandmothers of Plaza de Mayo, who campaign for the restoration of young people whose identities were stolen through abduction ('appropriation' is the word they use), originally estimated that there were nearly 600 children missing. The figure claimed is now closer to 400, and just over 100 have recovered their original family names, lost in forced adoptions. Last year, the Grandmothers published the figure of an additional 190 children who disappeared along with their parents.

When Reato's book was published, the statements appeared to some to be the first signal of an aged former president and army commander wanting to come clean with the country he had presided over for five years, or perhaps set the historical and numerical record straight. He even seemed to regret the terror. However, by May 2012, it was obvious that the ageing monster had agreed to talk on the record, first, to claim that he had been the boss; second, that he wanted to be seen as fully responsible for the military takeover and its actions; third, that he was proud of his role as a sort of saviour of the nation against the subversive menace (Marxist and nationalist Peronist guerrillas). For some, there was a brief hope that Videla was about to produce documents that recorded the military crimes (officially, they were destroyed in 1983, just before the elections, under orders of the last *de facto* chief, general Reynaldo Bignone, now in prison). But that idea was demolished by a letter from Videla to the conservative newspaper *La Nación*, published on 21 May, rejecting some of Reato's passages. Videla denies saying that seven or eight thousand 'had to die', but that, 'according to reliable figures, seven or eight thousand had died.'

It seemed a cop out. He further added: 'Mind, I do not regret a thing and I sleep soundly and at peace every night.'

General Jorge Videla, 1977
Credit: Rene Burri/Magnum

A mass grave near Cordoba, Argentina, found in October 2003
Credit: *Fer Arias/Photomasi/Camera Press*

Reato proved the former general wrong with pertinent transcripts from his 20 hours of interviews in handwritten notes (voice recorders and cameras are banned at the Campo de Mayo barracks where Videla is imprisoned), reprinted in *La Nación*. The roughs had been typed at home by Reato who on each subsequent visit to the prison took the typed sheets to Videla, who read and corrected by hand, and returned.

What had given the first inkling of hope for answers was Videla's death-toll figures. The 'seven or eight thousand' were not far from 'official' numbers, but distant from the 30,000 claimed by activist and human rights groups. Under President Raúl Alfonsín, the first civilian to be elected after the dictatorship in polls that were largely the result of the defeat of Argentina by Britain in the Falklands-Malvinas war in April–June 1982, it was agreed that there were 8,960 '*desaparecidos*' during the dictatorship, not including people killed in gun battles or armed attacks. This figure was recorded by a human rights group, known as Conadep (National

Commission on Disappeared Persons), that Dr Alfonsín appointed to compile the casualties list. This report led to the junta trials in 1985. The results were later confirmed in a book by Conadep secretary Graciela Fernández Meijide, at one time a national senator and the mother of a disappeared son. Years later, in 1991, in a private conversation held at a book launch, Dr Alfonsín accepted that totals found during his government could be projected to 14,000 maximum, to cover errors and omissions, but he would not accept the figure of 30,000. The initial total of dead, or disappeared, coincided with reports compiled by Amnesty International in London and by the Clamor human rights group in Brazil, in the 70s; it is also close to the figure posted on the national human rights secretariat web in 2009, under the current government of Cristina Kirchner – 7,954. The walls of the National Monument to the Victims of Terrorism, on the edge of the River Plate, list 8,875 names.

Speaking in her office a block away from the National Congress building, Senator Morandini was emphatic on her need, and by extension that of Argentina, to put human rights and the understanding of them above politics. 'And we've failed to do that for too long, which explains why some of our society can't or won't speak of the past, or argues that it is too long ago to carry on arguing or campaigning about events of the past. The trouble is we have not renewed our politics. Politics in Argentina were born dead at the end of the dictatorship. They have not changed style or discourse or policies from before the coup. We do not have politicians and parties that made sure a new political life was born to enhance democracy.

'We have had 30 years of democratic formalities and we do not have democratic values. This is because society has leaders who do not want to recognise their part or the role of their parties in the civic failure that led to the worst dictatorship in our history. Here people are still trying to convince themselves that we are a peaceful nation without admitting we were cutting each other's throats throughout the 19th century and killing people because we didn't like what they said in the 20th.

'We have not been able to see the difference between guilt and responsibility. Admiral Emilio Massera, commander of the navy during the dictatorship, and the most notorious of the tormentors, told the court in 1985, "I am responsible, but I do not feel guilty." He was speaking then as our politicians still try to make believe they can account for their decisions, but are not to blame for what goes wrong.' The US academic Marguerite Feitlowitz has a remarkable study of the linguistic twists of Admiral Massera in her book, *A Lexicon of Terror: Argentina and the Legacies of Torture.*

However, Norma Morandini has not lost hope for recovery. 'For the first time in decades we are beginning to look at ourselves, our own mistakes. This change is coming from a new generation, the youngest, the children, and even grandchildren of the activists, sometimes utopian, and the disappeared of the 70s. This makes me feel we are on our way to a political culture that includes responsibility. At present we still have many old habits. We look at the crises in Europe and delight in their suffering, seeing it as a failure. What we don't see in their plight is that the protesters are demanding more democracy.'

This is what Norma Morandini's deeply personal essay is about: the need for understanding loss, with the admission that she was greatly inspired by Hannah Arendt's writings: 'We must see others now as we want to see ourselves, with understanding. We need a greater sense of self-compassion, coming to terms with the intimacy of pain suffered. For me to say this, now, is to come to terms with the guilt I have felt, the guilt of being older than my brother and sister who were disappeared. My political activism was lightweight, theirs was committed, dangerous. I saw the sadness of my mother and how she recovered and grew to an admirable strength. As a society, now, we must understand that the formulation of our past to ourselves will be the means by which we handle our present and even our future. We have to find a balance somewhere between being sucked down into evil which destroys us and choosing departure, escape, which robs us of the humanity needed to understand. It is a difficult balance. The book has "washed my soul" as the Brazilians say. We must try to learn the concept that one man is all men, the behaviour of one belongs to us all.' ❏

©Andrew Graham-Yooll
41(3): 154/162
DOI: 10.1177/0306422012456134
www.indexoncensorship.org

Andrew Graham-Yooll is a journalist and writer who lives in Argentina. He was editor of *Index on Censorship* between 1989 and 1993. He was the editor of the English-language daily *Buenos Aires Herald* until 2007, and is now ombudsman at the newspaper *Perfil*

Soldiers conducting searches following the coup, 1976
Credit: SIPA PRESS/Rex Features

PROTAGONIST OF HISTORY

Ceferino Reato had many questions for junta dictator General Videla. He explains below how he secured 20 hours of exclusive interviews

'The phrase Final Solution was never used. The words Final Disposal were used frequently: those are two very military words that mean taking out of service something that is useless. When, for example, you speak of old clothing that is no longer used or worn out, it is marked Final Disposal. That has no further useful life.' Another of his remarks was: 'Let us assume that there were seven or eight thousand people who had to die to win the war against subversion: we could not execute them. Neither could we bring them to court.'

Twice before starting work on this book I had interviewed Jorge Rafael Videla. It became obvious that his remarks on the war against the guerrilla groups in the 70s were unknown, his views precise, sweeping and harsh. I shelved other plans to concentrate on *Final Disposal*.

There are questions that have pursued me for years, just as they must have so many other Argentines: when, how, where and why did the military take the decision to kill and disappear so many people? Why weren't they taken before a judge or executed? How did the military come to think that such an absence would be forgotten? Why were they taken to detention in secret places? How was torture to be justified? What was the influence of the so-called French Doctrine [a reference to the anti-guerrilla tactics imposed by the French army during the war of independence in Algeria, including extreme torture]? Do they have regrets? Was it a unanimous decision by the leadership of the armed forces? What was Videla's role? Is there a list of the victims? Where are their remains? How did the military refer among themselves to the circumstances? Could the lower rank officers disobey their orders? Did any disobey? Who, how, when and where was the Final Disposal decided for each of the detained? Was there a systematic plan to steal the children from the detained and hand them over to families that changed their identity? If that happened, why were there so many children appropriated by families linked to the military regime?

Final Disposal includes the testimony of other military chiefs, former officers, political appointees, guerrillas, politicians, trade unionists and businessmen who helped construct a picture as detailed as possible of those years of terror.

A visit to Montevideo helped to launch my project. Bookstores in the Uruguayan capital stocked copies with the self-criticism of former guerrillas, self-critical military officers, and reflections by the Tupamaros guerrillas on the dictatorship. There was one book based on interviews with general Gregorio Alvarez, Uruguay's Videla. I had previously tried and failed to interview the leader of the Montoneros guerrillas, Mario Eduardo Firmenich (sentenced to 30 years in prison, in a 1984 trial in which Andrew Graham-Yooll was prosecution witness at the request of President Raúl Alfonsín; pardoned in 1990 by President Carlos Menem), but I was able to speak to his second-in-command, Roberto Perdía. That interview, with Perdía and others of his kind, was what convinced Videla. 'To me, you are a protagonist of history,' I told Videla as we started our first interview on Wednesday, 26 October 2011. Videla smiled, unbelieving. The book is not a biography, but centred strongly on the concept of Videla as an historic character, the dictator during five out of the seven years and eight months that the military regime lasted.

Videla was the army strongman and head of a dictatorship different to all that came before; one that was much more violent, which sought to 'discipline an anarchic society' and launch 'a new economic model' which would liberate Argentina from the 'plagues' that prevented the country from reaching its manifest destiny. The plagues were seen to be Perónism, whose 'demagogic populism' was unbeatable in elections; trade unionism, which was an 'exaggerated and irrational' element of power; the land-owning bourgeoisie that had substituted hard, creative and competitive work with accommodation with whoever happened to be in government, through corruption and official credit that was never paid. All were seen as affected by the 'divisive and foreign oriented' line of the left in politics, trade unions and, above all, culture. This foundational objective was made clear in the baptism of the military regime, the National Reorganisation Process.

In this way, Videla represented the high point of the political and social autonomy of the army, and by extension the armed forces, which had grown since 1930. The counterpoint to this was the systematic decline of the parties and of all institutions of liberal, republican democracy. Thus, the army and the Catholic Church, the sword and the cross, united to defend the Fatherland and 'western and Christian' values. Videla was the main actor in the 24 March 1976 coup, which had the support of a vast majority of Argentines for multiple reasons, among them the bombings, the kidnappings, the hold-ups and hijackings, and the murders by the guerrillas. And it was also welcomed by groups that banked on a 'popular war' against the 'system's military machine', as Mario Eduardo Firmenich had stated in 1977 when opening a training course for cadres in the Montonero party.

Videla described each 'disappearance' as the 'disguising of a death' and explained why the forces resorted to that definition. 'The effort required to win the war was tremendous.'

The late author Ernesto Sabato in his original 1984 introduction (rewritten by President Néstor Kirchner in 2005) to the *Nunca Más* (Never Again) report by the National Commission on Disappeared Persons, Conadep, wrote: 'Thousands and thousands of human beings, generally young and even adolescent, became part of that terrifying and ghostly category: the "*Desaparecidos*". The word – a sorry Argentine privilege – is now used in Spanish in the press of all the world.'

A majority of the deaths, disappearances and thefts of children took place during the early stages of Videla's presidency, when he was also army chief. That fact alone would justify a book of interviews with Videla. After the return of democracy in December 1983, the former dictator was sentenced to life in prison and cashiered, banned from using rank and uniform. That was on 9 December 1985, at the end of the historic trial of the members of the first three military juntas. Five years later president Carlos Menem pardoned Videla, along with other officers and ministers, and the Montonero 'commander' Mario Firmenich. Videla lost his freedom again in 1998, accused of the theft of babies [of the 'disappeared']. He spent 38 days in prison and the courts conceded house arrest at his three-room home in the suburb of Belgrano (even the politicians and officers who detest him admit he made no money while in power). House arrest is granted to detainees over the age of 70, largely because the prison system is not designed to tend to people of that age. But it does depend on the judge. Ten years later, when Videla turned 83, a federal judge sent him to a military prison in the Campo de Mayo barracks, west of Buenos Aires.

President Menem's 1990 pardons were cancelled in part by congress and the supreme court during the presidency of the late Nestor Kirchner, on grounds that crimes against humanity could not be pardoned. Videla was tried again and sentenced on 22 December 2010, this time for the murder of 30 political prisoners held in Córdoba, between April and October 1976. His lawyers appealed.

Videla considers himself a political prisoner: 'I have been tried for all actions during the war against subversion in the trials of 1985. In some I was found guilty, I was absolved of other charges. The new trials have no meaning because nobody can be tried twice for the same actions. Also, my accusers are using legislation concerning *lesa humanidad* (crimes against humanity) that was passed after the events I am accused of.'

He was not a 'classic' dictator given his personality and because military power was divided. There was a junta, formed by the commanders of the army, navy and air force, which in theory stood above the office of president. The public administration was carved up between the three forces, each controlling part of the bureaucracy, although hampered by a complex system of veto and cross-checks involving the other forces.

'I was not a typical dictator, Pinochet style, for organic reasons, given that supreme power was divided in three. And I have not been an authoritarian. Certainly, I was a dictator in the Roman sense, as a temporary remedy, to save the institutions of the republic. I would have preferred not to have been so. I would rather have not had to save those institutions. But I was a military officer who did his duty, who took over government as an act of service.' Videla considered that nobody conditioned his rule. 'Truth is, during five years I did as I wished. Nobody hampered my government; not the junta or anybody else.' He admitted his decisive responsibility in the methods used under the Final Disposal.

I was a dictator in the Roman sense, as a temporary remedy

From one point of view it is practical to consider Videla, Massera, Firmenich, Perdía and others as the protagonists of history; convenient, because it frees us – the public, journalists, politicians – of the prejudices and passions that such figures spark, and releases an interviewer from asking nice, polite questions, insisting on clarification if necessary, and from looking at personality details or the way the interviewee lives.

However, some of those sources appear more than eager to be interviewed. On the warm night of Friday, 11 March 2011, I went to the home of General Albano Harguindeguy, Videla's once powerful and terrifying interior (home) minister, on a street ironically named Eva Perón in a suburb of Buenos Aires. The 'Basque' as his second wife, Elena, calls him, is under house arrest and awaited me in his wheelchair.

Harguindeguy answered all my questions, his memory intact, his glance clear and cunning, his voice at once friendly and ironic, even if a little dulled by age. The government of Cristina Kirchner and followers were marking

Photographs of people who disappeared during Argentina's 1976–83 military dictatorship
Credit: Marcos Brindicci/Reuters

the 38th anniversary of the election victory of Juan Perón's delegated presidential candidate, a dentist and former national deputy named Héctor J Cámpora (who was removed 49 days after taking office by the man who had made him presidential candidate, Juan Perón). At 11pm, when the interview was over, Harguindeguy remarked: 'They thought they were omnipotent. We believed we were omnipotent.' I thanked him. 'You can't leave already,' he complained. 'Hardly anybody visits me these days.'

I thought that we journalists were doing something wrong, writing more than necessary about the 70s. And yet we do not consult the actors of those years enough: the military are in prison or at home. Defeated, sentenced, bored, abandoned by their successors in command, many of them are available and ready to answer questions about the past.

That was the case with Videla, who started to end 'the silence I had forced on myself' from about mid-2010. He first spoke out at his trial in Córdoba. Next he granted an interview to the Spanish weekly *Cambio 16*, published in two parts, on 12 February and 4 March 2012. Ten days after this coverage, which won wide notice in Argentina because of his criticism of the Kirchner government, I found him in great spirits. Videla, like many of his imprisoned peers, had gambled on the defeat of Cristina Kirchner in the October 2011 presidential elections. He had really expected a former president, Eduardo Duhalde, to win, and then he would have been freed by a special amnesty. After the 54 per cent re-election victory secured by President Cristina Kirchner for another four years, Videla concluded that at his age there was no point in refusing to be interviewed. That may have been the reason he first granted an interview to *Cambio 16* magazine. The debate as to whether or not journalists should interview characters such as Videla remains open.

For human rights organisations in Argentina and followers of the Kirchners, the demons were Videla, the military and police during the dictatorship. Therefore, the guerrillas, the activists, were angels: young people filled with enthusiasm, fervour and pure ideals sacrificed their lives for a better Argentina, where there would be real freedom and equality. As if such noble aims can gloss over some of the methods used which were in clear violation of human rights. The undercurrent in the official view now is that there is a moral superiority on the left and amongst revolutionaries. This counters the view of the 80s, when people spoke of two forms of terrorism: on the left, the guerrillas, on the right, the state. 'The two demons' was the definition then. In fact, the basic ideas of the left are currently shared by the right. They differ only in some of the language: the left speaks of the working classes and socialism. The right refers to patriotism and nationalism.

But the violence of the dictatorship cannot be equated with that of the guerrilla groups: it is not just the number of casualties. The Final Disposal was particularly vehement because it was implemented as a policy of the state, in theory the guarantor of law and life in society.

As a result of the theory of 'angels and demons', human rights organisations and the government insist that the number of *desaparecidos* is 30,000, even though official figures range from 7,500 to 8,875 'disappeared' and confirmed deaths, named and identified, and even though those figures include some killed as far back as 1969. Videla speaks of 'seven or eight thousand' people 'who had to be killed' although, in a strange coincidence with one progressive group, he remarked, 'we could argue the figures', but the key element 'is not in the numbers but the fact'.

It is not a minor issue. The Argentine state should be concerned with establishing an exact number, not just because 30 years after the return of

Mothers of Plaza de Mayo, the relatives of the disappeared, demand justice, Buenos Aires, 1985
Credit: Julio Etchart/Alamy

democracy it is time to know the truth in all areas. One way of closing old wounds would be to find out what happened with each of the disappeared or, at least, the whereabouts of their remains. That would be basic in mitigating the pain of their loved ones who have no place to leave a flower. President Cristina Kirchner was right to say that 'there must be no greater horror for the human condition than that uncertainty'. Disappearance implies a double death.

But it is difficult to know the whereabouts of the disappeared, all of them, without a list of names and figures as precise as possible. Arguing at this stage that victims of the dictatorship were 30,000 makes the problem of finding their remains unsolvable. It is a banner for the politics of human rights, but no more.

Videla occupies cell number 5 in the military prison. It is a small room. There is a single bed with a wine-red cover stretched very tidily. There is a crucifix on the wall above the pillow, a small wardrobe, a fan, a heater and a dressing table on which stands a photo of his wife when she was 15. Mrs Alicia Raquel Hartridge de Videla can hardly walk, but visits him each week. There are blue curtains on the single window. The toilet and shower are shared with the prisoner next door. There is a chapel nearby where Videla prays every day at 7pm. On Sundays he takes communion. He is convinced God always guided him and never let go of his hand, not even in prison.

As we parted I had to say: 'You will not be satisfied with this book, because that is inevitable. Given the subjects we have discussed, the only way you could like a book is if you or some friend writes it.' ❑

©Ceferino Reato
41(3): 163/172
DOI: 10.1177/0306422012456138
www.indexoncensorship.org

These are edited extracts from the introduction to Final Disposal *(Disposición Final) by Ceferino Reato, translated from Spanish by Andrew Graham-Yooll. The book is published by Sudamericana, Buenos Aires*

index
on CENSORSHIP

volume 7   number 3
May-June 1978

THE SIN OF POWER

Power not only distorts reality but seeks to convince people that the false is true.
Arthur Miller on the struggle for rights from East to West

It is always necessary to ask how old a writer is who is reporting his impressions of a social phenomenon. Like the varying depth of a lens, the mind bends the light passing through it quite differently according to its age. When I first experienced Prague in the late 60s, the Russians had only just entered with their armies; writers (almost all of them self-proclaimed Marxists if not Party members) were still unsure of their fate under the new occupation, and when some 30 or 40 of them gathered in the office of *Listy* to 'interview' me, I could smell the apprehension among them. And indeed, many would soon be fleeing abroad, some would be jailed, and others would never again be permitted to publish in their native language. Incredibly, that was almost a decade ago.

But since the first major blow to the equanimity of my mind was the victory of Nazism, first in Germany and later in the rest of Europe, the images I have of repression are inevitably cast in fascist forms. In those times the communist was always the tortured victim, and the Red Army stood as the hope of man, the deliverer. So to put it quite simply, although correctly, I think, the occupation of Czechoslovakia was the physical proof that Marxism was but one more self-delusionary attempt to avoid facing the real nature of power, the primitive corruption by power of those who possess it. In a word, Marxism has turned out to be a form of sentimentalism toward human nature, and this has its funny side. After all, it was initially a probe into the most painful wounds of the capitalist presumptions, it was scientific and analytical.

What the Russians have done in Czechoslovakia is, in effect, to prove in a western cultural environment that what they have called socialism simply cannot tolerate even the most nominal independent scrutiny, let alone an opposition. The critical

Warsaw Pact troops invade Prague, August 1968
Credit: Josef Koudelka/Magnum

intelligence itself is not to be borne, and in the birthplace of Kafka and of the absurd in its subtlest expression absurdity emanates from the Russian occupation like some sort of gas which makes one both laugh and cry. Shortly after returning home from my first visit to Prague mentioned above, I happened to meet a Soviet political scientist at a high-level conference where he was a participant representing his country and I was invited to speak at one session to present my views of the impediments to better cultural relations between the two nations. Still depressed by my Czech experience, I naturally brought up the invasion of the country as a likely cause for American distrust of the Soviets, as well as the United States aggression in Vietnam from the same detente viewpoint.

That had been in the morning; in the evening at a party for all the conference participants, half of them Americans, I found myself facing this above-mentioned Soviet whose anger was unconcealed. 'It is amazing,' he said, 'that you — especially you as a Jew — should attack our action in Czechoslovakia.' Normally quite alert to almost any reverberations of the Jewish presence in the political life of our time,

I found myself in a state of unaccustomed and total confusion at this remark, and I asked the man to explain the connection. 'But obviously,' he said (and his face had gone quite red and he was quite furious now) 'we have gone in there to protect them from the West German fascists.'

I admit that I was struck dumb. Imagine! The marching of all the Warsaw Pact armies in order to protect the few Jews left in Czechoslovakia! It is rare that one really comes face to face with such fantasy so profoundly believed by a person of intelligence. In the face of this kind of expression all culture seems to crack and collapse; there is no longer a frame of reference.

In fact, the closest thing to it that I could recall were my not infrequent arguments with intelligent supporters or apologists for our Vietnamese invasion. But at this point the analogy ends, for it was always possible during the Vietnam war for Americans opposed to it to make their views heard, and, indeed, it was the widespread opposition to the war which finally made it impossible for President Johnson to continue in office. It certainly was not a simple matter to oppose the war in any significant way, and the civilian casualties of protest were by no means few, and some – like the students at the Kent State College protest – paid with their lives. But what one might call the unofficial underground reality, the version of morals and national interest held by those not in power, was ultimately expressed and able to prevail sufficiently to alter high policy. Even so, it was the longest war ever fought by Americans.

Any discussion of the American rationales regarding Vietnam must finally confront something which is uncongenial to both Marxist and anti-Marxist viewpoints, and it is the inevitable pressure, by those holding political power, to distort and falsify the structures of reality. The Marxist, by philosophical conviction, and the bourgeois American politician, by practical witness, both believe at bottom that reality is quite simply the arena into which determined men can enter and reshape just about every kind of relationship in it. The conception of an objective reality which is the summing up of all historical circumstances, as well as the idea of human beings as containers or vessels by which that historical experience defends itself and expresses itself through common sense and unconscious drives, are notions which at best are merely temporary nuisances, incidental obstructions to the wished for remodelling of human nature and the improvements of society which power exists in order to set in place.

The sin of power is to not only distort reality but to convince people that the false is true, and that what is happening is only an invention of enemies. Obviously, the Soviets and their friends in Czechoslovakia are by no means the only ones guilty of this sin, but in other places, especially in the West, it is possible yet for witnesses to reality to come forth and testify to the truth. In Czechoslovakia the whole field is pre-empted by the power itself.

Demonstrators mourn the victims of the Kent State massacre on 4 May 1970, Boston Common
Credit: Spencer Gray/Alamy

Thus a great many people outside, and among them a great many artists, have felt a deep connection with Czechoslovakia – but precisely because there has been a fear in the West over many generations that the simple right to reply to power is a tenuous thing and is always on the verge of being snipped like a nerve. I have, myself, sat at dinner with a Czech writer and his family in his own home and looked out and seen police sitting in their cars down below, in effect warning my friend that our 'meeting' was being observed. I have seen reports in Czech newspapers that a certain writer had emigrated to the West and was no longer willing to live in his own country, when the very same man was sitting across a living-room coffee table from me. And I have also been lied about in America by both private and public liars, by the press and the government, but a road – sometimes merely a narrow path – always remained open before my mind, the belief that I might sensibly attempt to influence people to see what was real and so at least to resist the victory of untruth.

I know what it is to be denied the right to travel outside my country, having been denied my passport for some five years by our Department of State. And I know a little about the inviting temptation to simply get out at any cost, to quit my country in disgust and disillusion, as no small number of people did in the McCarthy 50s and as a long line of Czechs and Slovaks have in these recent years. I also know the empty feeling in the belly at the prospect of trying to learn another nation's secret language, its gestures and body communications without which a writer is only half-seeing and half-hearing. More important, I know the conflict between recognising the indifference of the people and finally conceding that the salt has indeed lost its savour and that the only sensible attitude toward any people is cynicism.

So that those who have chosen to remain as writers on their native soil despite remorseless pressure to emigrate are, perhaps no less than their oppressors, rather strange and anachronistic figures in this time. After all, it is by no means a heroic epoch now; we in the West as well as in the East understand perfectly well that the political and military spheres – where 'heroics' were called for in the past – are now merely expressions of the unmerciful industrial-technological base. As for the very notion of patriotism, it falters before the perfectly obvious interdependence of the nations, as well as the universal prospect of mass obliteration by the atom bomb, the instrument which has doomed us, so to speak, to this lengthy peace between the great powers.

That a group of intellectuals should persist in creating a national literature on their own ground is out of tune with our adaptational proficiency which has flowed from these developments. It is hard anymore to remember whether one is living in Rome or New York, London or Strasbourg, so homogenised has western life become. The persistence of these people may be an inspiration to some but a nuisance to others, and not only inside the oppressing apparatus but in the West as well. For these so-called dissidents are apparently upholding values at a time when the first order of business would seem to be the accretion of capital for technological investment.

It need hardly be said that by no means everybody in the West is in favour of human rights, and western support for eastern dissidents has more hypocritical self-satisfaction in it than one wants to think too much about. Nevertheless, if one has learned anything at all in the past 40 or so years, it is that to struggle for these rights (and without them the accretion of capital is simply the construction of a more modern prison) one has to struggle for them wherever the need arises.

That this struggle also has to take place in socialist systems suggests to me that the fundamental procedure which is creating violations of these rights transcends social systems – a thought anathematic to Marxists but possibly true nevertheless. What may be in place now is precisely a need to erect a new capital structure, be it in Latin America or the Far East or underdeveloped parts of Europe, and just as in the 19th century in America and England it is a process which always breeds injustice and the flaunting of human spiritual demands because it essentially is the sweating of increasing amounts of production and wealth from a labour force surrounded, in effect, by police. The complaining or reforming voice in that era was not exactly encouraged in the United States or England; by corrupting the press and buying whole legislatures, capitalists effectively controlled their opposition, and the struggle of the trade union movement was often waged against firing rifles.

One has to struggle for these rights wherever the need arises

There is of course a difference now, many differences. At least they are supposed to be differences, particularly that the armed force is in the hands of a state calling itself socialist and progressive and scientific, no less pridefully than the 19th-century capitalisms boasted by their Christian ideology and their devotion to the human dimension of political life as announced by the American Bill of Rights and the French Revolution. But the real difference now is the incomparably deeper and more widespread conviction that man's fate is not 'realistically' that of the regimented slave. It may be that despite everything, and totally unannounced and unheralded, a healthy scepticism toward the powerful has at last become second nature to the great mass of people almost everywhere. It may be that history, now, is on the side of those who hopelessly hope and cling to their native ground to claim it for their language and ideals.

The oddest request I ever heard in Czechoslovakia – or anywhere else – was to do what I could to help writers publish their works – but not in French, German or English, the normal desire of sequestered writers cut off from the outside. No, these Czech writers were desperate to see their works in Czech! Somehow this speaks of something far more profound than 'dissidence' or any political quantification. There is something like love in it, and in this sense it is a prophetic yearning and demand. ◻

©1977 by Arthur Miller
41(3): 173/180
DOI: 10.1177/0306422012438318
www.indexoncensorship.org